THE BEST AU

POEMS

20
16

THE BEST AUSTRALIAN
POEMS

20
16

EDITED BY SARAH HOLLAND-BATT

Black Inc.

Published by Black Inc.,
an imprint of Schwartz Publishing Pty Ltd
Level 1, 221 Drummond Street
Carlton VIC 3053, Australia
enquiries@blackincbooks.com
www.blackincbooks.com

ISBN: 9781863958875 (pbk)
ISBN: 9781925435351 (ebook)

Cover design by Peter Long
Typesetting by Tristan Main

Printed in Australia by McPherson's Printing Group.

FSC
www.fsc.org
MIX
Paper from
responsible sources
FSC® C001695

Contents

Introduction

'I SEE THE POET AS A SEISMOGRAPH OF THE AGE'S DARKER regions,' Fay Zwicky wrote in a recently published extract of her journals.* 'Living out fifty years of this dreadful century has certainly made the needle twitch without stopping.' I have turned Zwicky's enigmatic, quaking metaphor of the seismograph over in my mind since I read it; in it, I recognise two ideas. The first is that while the poet does not leap at every cataclysmic event or operate as some kind of geopolitical tuning fork, she often responds powerfully to the dark events and anxieties of the age. Poetry is not written in a vacuum: it is of its time, and it responds to the conditions of its time – whether earnestly or satirically, directly or aslant. And, like a seismograph, the poet often registers the uneasy vibrations of a culture before the repercussions are felt by the body politic – a dangerous prescience that goes some way toward explaining why poets are persecuted by authoritarian regimes the world over.

But Zwicky's metaphor also speaks more broadly to poetry's curious relationship to time. As a form, poetry is paradoxically both fleeting and ephemeral, yet remarkably durable. It is able to respond nimbly to its subject matter, at lightning speed – yet last, at its best, for millennia afterwards. It inhabits the language of the hour, and often of the minute; we see this in its swift and often parodic adoption of neologisms, its linguistic dexterity and adaptability, its unceasing and energetic reinvention – yet its readers enjoy decoding it centuries later. The poet, like the seismograph, skitters over the peaks and troughs of a lifetime,

*Dougan, Lucy and Zwicky, Fay. "Plain Speech: Extracts from Fay Zwicky's Journals."*Axon: Creative Explorations* 5.2 (Nov 2015)

but the poem itself is a series of aftershocks realised through generations of readers who follow.

This durability is precisely because the poem detonates in the instant of its reading. Its utterances come into being just as we vault each enjambment; its silences and spaces are conjured up in the moment we encounter them; its meaning is arrived upon through the jouissance and play of reading. Above all, poetry – for both its readers and its writers – is a form that demands attentiveness and active intelligence. It treats language as a volatile and charged commodity, and one whose subtleties and nuances are worth puzzling over. As Valéry defined it, poetry is 'a separate language, or more specifically, a language within a language'. In the context of our increasingly corrosive political discourse and the fuzzy 'truthiness' that pervades it, poetry seems to me a radical form, and reading it a radical act.

Reading the past year's poetry with a view to editing this anthology was a different species of reading than I am used to – full of the usual exhilarating jolts of delight and surprise, but accompanied by an unusual anxiety. I found myself charmed and elated by some poems one day, but then a little cool on them the next; they looked different in one light than they did in another. I wanted to be sure of the poems, but found myself returning to a favourite Michael Dransfield poem more than once, with renewed understanding:

> i'm not dead
> sure of the poems
>
> life seems
> to suffer a bit
>
> in the translation

Like Dransfield, I was 'not dead / sure of the poems'. I circled back, re-reading and re-reading, feeling like a forensic scientist must: on the hunt for proof, for certainty. I reminded myself that reading poetry – and the joy of a particular poem – is a sort of alchemy; at the risk of sounding mystical, there are aspects to the reading experience that seem mercurial, quixotic, dependent on some unpredictable internal weather. Some days, the poem's electric power, its frisson, can 'suffer a bit / in the translation'.

So I re-read, patiently – obsessively is probably the more accurate adverb – and slowly a magnetic group of poems emerged that I found myself returning to, over and over again. Their shocks, to paraphrase a line from a superb Lucy Dougan poem included in this selection, went right through me. I turned them to the light many times, probing their facets; they emerged from this process adamantine. Lines from each of them are now lodged permanently in my mind, and I am as sure of these poems as I am of anything.

I aimed to capture a diverse cross section of the poetry being written in Australia at present and to include the work of new poets wherever I could, but above all I paid attention to the individual poems themselves, privileging those that seemed most urgent, startling, stylish, ingenious, defiant, alive. My selection gestures towards the formal and thematic variety and brilliant inventiveness of our poets, but is a beginning rather than an end point in that respect. Overall, I was struck by the sheer volume of extraordinary poems being published in Australia, the dynamism and range of our poets. I was also struck by the dedication of our poetry editors and anthologists. If, as Dransfield once wrote, 'to be a poet in Australia / is the ultimate commitment', then the work of poetry editors and publishers verges on zealotry of the best sort.

There are several projects and anthologies that stood out over my past year of reading that are worth remarking on; I hope readers of this anthology will seek them out. *Australian Book Review* introduced a new initiative with States of Poetry – a significant new annual anthology drawing attention to the geographic distribution and localities of our poets. Dan Disney and Kit Kelen co-edited *Writing to the Wire*, a remarkable and urgent anthology centred on refugee and asylum seeker issues.

Bonny Cassidy and Jessica Wilkinson co-edited the recently published Hunter Anthology of *Contemporary Australian Feminist Poetry* – a fantastically rich and diverse collection that introduced me to several emerging poets I have included here. And Kate Fagan and Ann Vickery co-edited the excellent *Active Aesthetics: Contemporary Australian Poetry*, a significant anthology collecting poets committed to decolonisation, ecopoetics, cultural unsettlement, and other forms of transformational poetics.

One of the great pleasures of Australian poetry is its quality of sprawl, to borrow Les Murray's phrase. The poems collected here sprawl geographically – from the 'pimple amongst the wildflowers' of the colonial township at Mullewa in Charmaine Papertalk-Green's eclogue with John Kinsella, to the catfish hole at Jayipa in Phillip Hall's 'Royalty' and the crustacean effigy at Ballina in Fiona Hile's 'Relocation of the Big Prawn'. In a country where even the names of so many of our literary journals signal towards geographical orientation or locality – *Meanjin, Overland, Southerly, Island, Westerly* – it is perhaps unsurprising that many of these poems contend with place. But their sprawl extends beyond national borders, and is wholly cosmopolitan, veering to the glacial tip of South America in Maria Takolander's 'Argument', a Norwegian graveyard in Kit Kelen's 'takk for alt,' a Guangzhou wet market in Lachlan Brown's 'Suspended Belief', Biscayan and Tahitian surf breaks in Jaya Savige's 'Hossegor', and Rome's ancient sewerage system in Elizabeth Campbell's 'Cloaca Maxima'. The worldliness and urbanity of these peripatetic poems will surely strike readers as a refreshing palate cleanser from the parochialism, tribalism and nativism dominating much of our political discourse at present.

Beyond their terrestrial ambulations, the poems in this year's anthology also sprawl across a dazzlingly diverse range of subjects and aesthetics. There are poems that tremor with the anxieties of the war on terror, with the seismic shifts of Brexit and the promise of Grexit, poems that reverberate with social and cultural discontent and unsettlement. There are poems that probe news events frequently shrouded by cultural amnesia – from Ali Cobby

Eckermann's indelible 'Black Deaths in Custody' to Michelle Cahill's 'Car Lover', a haunting address to those who assault and murder women. There are poems centred on the body – its precariousness, its sensuality, its limitations and mortality – and poems about the often disturbing advances in biotechnology. There are poems sketching the relationship between the human and natural worlds that fizz with a particularly muscular Australian vernacular – Les Murray's native bees as evicted smallholders 'with their new life to rebuild, / new eggs, new sugarbag, // gold skinfulls of water', or Judith Beveridge's corpulent toads 'bull[ing] their way across earth'. There are poems interrogating the nexus between language, place, and belonging, stretching from those charting migrant experiences in our capital cities, such as Omar Sakr's 'ghosting the ghetto' and π.o.'s 'Shakespeare & the State Library', to the memorable 'Learning Buandjalung on Tharawal' by Evelyn Araluen – a powerful account of the continuous cultural knowledge embedded in language and Country.

One of the most likeable aspects of contemporary Australian poetry is that it is profane as often as it is sacred; there is a rich vein of irony and satire that runs through our poetics, a colloquialism, contrarianism and playfulness that separates it from its counterparts in the northern hemisphere. This enduring quality is evident in many of the poems collected here, including brilliant contributions by Pam Brown, John Tranter, Ken Bolton, Ouyang Yu, Jill Jones and Tim Thorne. There are poems that respond ekphrastically to other art forms, from Jessica L. Wilkinson's 'FAUNE et JEUX' to Bronwyn Lea's playful encounter with the kitsch porn aesthetics of pop art superstar Jeff Koons, and those that speak to the act of writing itself, such as Robert Adamson's intertextual 'Black Winged Stilts', with its Stevensian 'mangrove tree at the end of the mind', or Andy Kissane's sardonic take on recent plagiarism scandals in 'Getting away with it'. Overall, I suspect my selection skews slightly darker in tone than some previous years; this perhaps speaks to the fact that the past year has felt a particularly vertiginous one. These poems speak in and of unsettling times; in the maelstrom, they shudder and catch.

The anthology this year opens with an emblematic poem by the late poet Martin Harrison, 'Patio', from his stunning last book, *Happiness*: just as the patio itself serves as entryway to the house, so Harrison's poem is the entry point to the past year's poems. As well as being one of our finest poets, scholars and environmentalists, Harrison was an indefatigable mentor and teacher to many of the poets in this anthology, and I encourage those readers and admirers of his work to seek out the edition of *Plumwood Mountain*, guest edited by Stuart Cooke and Peter Minter, dedicated to his memory. 'Patio' is, among other things, an entreaty to remember our capacity for wonder in the face of so much darkness – a fitting inclusion from a poet who brought wonder and delight to so many of his readers and fellow writers.

Bookending the collection this year is an arresting last poem by Billy Marshall Stoneking, another generous mentor and vital member of the Australian poetry community, who passed away during the parentheses of this anthology's timeframe. Stoneking was a poet, playwright, scriptwriter and producer who had a keen interest in Indigenous issues since he first arrived in Australia in the 1970s, and spent an extended period of time living in the Papunya Aboriginal Settlement, where he helped found a literacy program to empower local Luritja and Pintupi peoples to read and write their own languages. His haunting 'One Last Poem' speaks to his enduring interest in language preservation in the Northern Territory; it is a poem that gave me chills when I discovered it, and I know it will do the same for readers of this anthology.

This past year, the Australian poetry community also lost Dimitris Tsaloumas, a brilliant and humane poet whose work I have loved for as long as I have been a reader of Australian poetry. There have been many wonderful tributes to him by those who knew him best, including Vrasidas Karalis in the *Sydney Review of Books*, Helen Nickas in *Australian Poetry Journal* and Antigone Kefala in *Rochford Street Review*; these essays speak not only to his superb poetry but also to his seminal work in translation and the way in which his writing, while always highly regarded by peers and critics, has been somewhat neglected due to his position as a poet of the Greek diaspora; as Nickas writes, 'Tsaloumas remained largely an outsider in Australia.' This neglect does a great disservice to his exceptional body of poems; I am sure that future generations of readers, poets and critics will return to his oeuvre and see his extraordinary contribution to Australian literature.

Due to his ailing health, Tsaloumas was unable to write in his last years, which is why I could not represent him within the pages of this anthology with a recent poem. Instead, he will have the last say of this introduction, via lines from one of his best-loved poems, 'Note With Interlude From the Banks of The Brisbane in September', first published in his classic volume *Falcon Drinking*. The poem begins with the poet sitting beside a 'fawn-thick' Brisbane River that 'gifts a city with loveliness', prompting him to enter into a fantasia about 'days of happiness' with the hetaerae of Ancient Greece: a reverie brought about by a sudden visitation of poetry, of 'words come forth again, / unfathomable, out of yellow-paged time'. Here, Tsaloumas writes about the ways in which the poet's work – punctuated by delight and exuberance – is ultimately fleeting for the poet, beginning and ending in doubt. He reminds us, too, of the great gift poets leave behind for their readers, of the treasury of their enduring works. Tsaloumas, Stoneking and Harrison were all fine, original, necessary poets whose works reverberate with the concerns of their time; while their vital works and voices will endure, we will miss them in the years to come.

> I write because
> this ache gets sharper with the years
> and my truth is but a husk of substance
> wasted, my strength no longer adequate
> to breast the song of the rock-bound sisters.
> My message is this: in the old cupboard
> in the wall, beside the mirror
> opposite the bed, you'll find some papers
> held in a roll with string:

please burn them. Youthful,
possibly happy stuff, I can't recall –
things one could redeem perhaps
in leaner times, but burn them nonetheless.
This has been preying on my mind of late,
but if I am to end this journey at all
it'll have to be as I began, expecting nothing.

Sarah Holland-Batt

Patio

At any moment
any slice or gash,
a huge explosion falling
in any direction –

outside the window
a swatch of bladed leaves
sways this way that way
inside the frame:

wordless day bounces
down the tree's bare limbs,
through its outspread flamboyance
toward twigs and wattle-birds

while they maraud sticky cream flowers
as if beauty could be instantly
sucked from the world.
Directly. Without irony.

Martin Harrison

Black Winged Stilts

Two long, plaited, clouds of cotton-wool fog
Roll across exposed mudflats as tide runs in.
Morning sunlight bleeds an opaque water
Coloured script onto the tide— it sets loose
A word I discovered once in a poem
On Black Hawk Island: 'condensare'.

Scatterings of black winged stilts fly in
To make a landing on the bay. They are taller
Than the early spoonbills, royal ones,
A river's vanishing poets. The stilts slowly
Step forward, up to their bright pink knees in mud,
Spearing a crunchy breakfast as they go.

The black winged stilts keep a quick eye
On a lone human with a camera aimed at them.
Pictures dissolve, let's say images should
Disappear, like the poetry of birds—before
We invent a language for the final entry, before
The need for a sleek soul and a slim presence.

A black winged stilt is a loaded bow,
It's needle beak, the arrow. Lorine Niedecker
Called her writing room 'this condensery'
And said her trade was to sit at a desk and condense.
This occurred a while back, these days poets
Learn to muddy the page and expand.

Gathering bullhead memories in a seine net
The heaviest break through the mesh.
A mangrove tree at the end of the mind is draped
With her father's net, caught thoughts
Fade as slime dries in the sun. Minutes ago,
A line ago, the black winged stilts were wading,
Gathering spoonbill poems, yabbies, soldier crabs.

The birds have flown, taken their poems
Neatly tucked into a book, Judith Wright's 'Birds'
Forget the vanishing poets. Breathe life
Into hollow bones, take heart in backwater craft.
Carry language, a mullet's leaping joy, on your breath:
I have come to believe the black winged stilts
Carry knowledge of their particular death.

Robert Adamson

In The Billy Sing Baghdad Bar-and-Grill

I'd heard the director didn't need an Asian to play him,
young Billy Sing, Gallipoli's finest sniper.
After all our Kylie could play a geisha.
His Dad was a drover from Shanghai,
his mother Mary-Ann from Staffordshire.
Proud member, model minority hard
working, civil, didn't do anger or shout,
no doctor had to fix his face.
Essentially Us, a little whitewash
with a good spotter – a novelist.
Productive, liked good roast duck fried rice.
Could have met my ancestor, the Captain
who rode in the cavalry, sold beer,
was mayor of the city staffed with his progeny.
Strengths? At Gallipoli Sing bowled a long spell
under mortar bombardment.
Billie Sing shooting Turks by the hundreds,
brave but hardly suicidal –
no North Korean human wave bullshit,
the Bravery column balanced the Common Sense column.
Why give away your position?
Weaknesses: Sang-froid? Myalgia?
Who needs to know in the Billy Sing
Baghdad Bar-and-Grill.

Adam Aitken

⌐

—this light exists   —that dark
divides   —death clouds into   —Euclidean
space & locally   —compacts *I*
love you   —therefore the lemma
may   —may not be true

    this flame which burns this
    lamp which shines the logical
    constant in your eyes &
    linear truth that "light exists"
    I cannot confirm this proof

Jordie Albiston

Advanced Souvlaki

A kookaburra sits on the cage
at the top of the rusty stinkpole
with a neckless air of gravity.
A man with a spirit level trips.
The grandad caravan with its crown
of loudspeakers is back from Darwin.
If the question is still, What's the point
of anything at all? there's nothing
left to start to make an answer from.

Behind the cluttered yard that will be
three dark garage spaces for crickets
to stridulate in, a cottage squats.
The dead man's fingers are red in claw.
Pizza and scandalized reaction
are proffered in a mini-playground
with a massive sandstone portico.
It should have been abundantly clear
for some time now that you're with stupid.

It's the conference of the currawongs;
no ambulance can interrupt it.
Two fresh-faced Euro-canvassers tread
the narrow path to the hoarder's door.
In front of the gutted shop that was
Advanced Souvlaki, a rubber kid
tries his rabona kick on a stone
and ¡GOL! I can't fault those arguments
to justify despair. You know that.

Chris Andrews

Learning Bundjalung on Tharawal

> Above his desk it is written:
> 'I wish I knew the names of all the birds.'

I know this room through tessellation of leaf and branch,
wurahɲ-bil and *jaran-gir,*
in the shade of a *kulsetsi*—
  (Cherokee) 'honey locust' [a flowering tree].

> I am relearning these hills and saltwaters
> and all the places wrapped around this room
> We both have *dagahral* here,
> lovers/fathers/friends/conquerors/
> ghosts.

> But here, in this new and ancient place,
> I ask him to name the song that swoops through this mosaic:
> Sometimes it is wattlebird sometimes it is currawong—
> when we drive, he tells me king parrot, fairy wren, black
> cockatoo

and I know jalwahn and bilin bilin and ngarehr
  but the rest are just *nunganybil,*
  the rest are just: 'bird'

It is hard to unlearn a language:
  to unspeak the empire,
  to teach my voice to rise and fall like landscape,
a topographic intonation.

So in this place the shape of my place
I am trying to sing like hill and saltwater,
to use old words from an old country that I have never walked

on:
  bundjalung jagum ngai, nganduwal nyuyaya,
and god, I don't even know
        if I'm saying it right.

But I watch the bark twist:
grey and slate and vanilla and vermillion
        he tells me this is ribbon gum—
so I find five words for this bark
and I promise I will learn them all

                    Because to hold him is to hold the tree
                        that holds these birds I cannot name,
                            and a word spoken here
                        might almost sound like home.

We are relearning this place through poetry:
    I open my book and say, *wayan,*
here is a word which means road, but also root
and in it I am rooted, earthed,
singing between two lands
    I learn that *balun* is both river and milky way,
    and that he is *baray-gir,* the youngest child
    and the top of the tree,
    where the *gahr* will come to rest—
    to call its own name
    across the canopy,
    long after his word for it
    is gone.

Evelyn Araluen

A Panegyric for Toads

These slum-lords of burrows and tree-hollows
are on the move, dozens of pulsing lung-sacs
'a little ventriloquism of ducks' singing in the spring.

Folklore says the toad's a shape-shifter — rancour,
and primeval trouble in its head, devil-worship
on its tongue, its third eye-lid perpetually wiping

away the sight of ghosts. A toad will leave a glaze
of poison on your hand, but you can forgive
it for this — look at those copper-red eyes leasing

fire to the damp core of evening; listen to their calls
in the reeds like the low-plucked strings of ouds;
and how, sometimes, as if led by an unseen conductor,

sensing peril, the singing instantaneously stops.
At first their mating will look like a congregational
laying on of hands, whose purpose, you could

think, is not to spawn, but to heal their warts.
Some say toads are always belching, breaking
wind, eating each other's shed skin, but I'd happily

kiss a toad on her sombre, gargoylean mouth,
follow her gawky walk to the slime-scented pond
where she must climb over a thick layer

of frog-spawn, and scrumming indissolubly
with a group of males, an iron-lock embrace
they won't break for days, risk drowning for sex.

Unlike frogs, loaded with the rapid taut and release
of sling-shot legs, toads like us, must land-walk,
eat with short tongues, bull their way across earth.

Judith Beveridge

Dark Heart

I look in here—this
notebook—& see
the notes for the
last review I did,
& note—that I am
about to write another.
Tho I would rather
write something else.
I whistle bop a bit
try not to think
of the vast tide of crap
the exhibition represents,
check the sky: sere,
grey, pale up one end
of the street,
almost Neapolitan
at the other
(pale, but a distinct
blue, some
dark smudged stain
drifting over it,
much closer *to*
than the far blue
behind—blown,
in those paintings,
from a volcano
somewhere at hand—
almost like flak
in the old movies.
                        (Goya's
mantilla, & parasol—
& the rumour,

nothing lasts)

#

It makes the
sky darker too
an atmosphere
not a backdrop

#

a small figure
further down
Hindley Street
is crossing the road—
I recognize the coat
as much as the figure—
but who?

#

It is about time
I had a drink with Crab.

About time for a
lot of things.

What to do
about this art?

I whistle
'You're My Thrill'
the beginning
—but, whistling it,
I end up,

as always, with
the 'Perry Mason Theme'
(I *think*)
        (it is
so long since I have
heard it)

Instantly recognisable
when I was a kid.

I thought I
didn't like it—

now it seems I do
or something
cousin to it.
'You're My Thrill'.

Then
'Couldn't It Be You'—

I wonder
what the
connection is —

the key, the pattern,
somehow relates?

Its calming effect
when whistled.

                So,

resignation,
'getting on
with things'.

Hate to turn
a beautiful tune
into a tic, a
neurotic response
tho again, luckily,
it is only the
first few bars
I remember
this way,
the rest of the song
is safe,
unretrievable.

When I play it
I smile.

This art then,
what to do about it?
Inflated in scale,
naive, 'done' when
its theme is recognised
— like logos
for a moral
position.
As if the viewer
should tick a box
in approval
& move on
perhaps 'liking' it
on their facebook page.
(their 'mental' facebook page)

Does anybody
do that,
like it that much
that they could bother

to register this vote   (?)
their
'shared concern'?
I doubt it.
But then
I am whistling the
wrong tune.

I read in Denton Welch
(the *Journals*)

of some gypsies he hears
coming home from the pub
singing 'Bye Bye Blackbird'
1946
My father used
to sing that song.
I love it.
       The
opening notes
of the John
Coltrane version.
           My father
sang it often enough
for me to know the words.

Denton, near the end—

"Chopin pours over me from the wireless.
Nothing but this small picture will be left
of the day. Many years after, people may
be able to read then say, 'He was cold; he
watched the sunset; he ate a chocolate,' but
nothing more will be left to them."

Today I worried happily,
wrote stuff, 'asseverated',
was alive. It was supposed
to get cold—but it didn't.

Ken Bolton

Discovered in a rock pool

A star-shaped object rising up
out of the water – five
wavering arms, five
spokes of a chariot wheel, five
curved cylinders, at their centre
a cluster of grey barnacles, small pearls, a silver light,

the water that drips from them
heavy with salt, oxidized
incrustations. A star tiara
from a drowned mermaid, the wheel
of some vast chariot washed up.
And, as it breaks the surface, this sharp sudden

fragrance like plants left
too long in narrow vases, the water
like urine drained out of dried twigs.
The wheel is a ghost of a wheel.
The fiery chariot's return to
the kingdom of salt. And everything

shrinks and is less than a token
miniature apple, a walnut placed
as a skull-shaped offering on an
altar to placate the goddess of devouring.
Effigies stored in a rock pool.
This is surely someone's

childhood not mine. Such simple things
might be placation or destruction. Starfish
or a galaxy intact
as its detritus. Burnt out. Cooling off,

cooling off in a solution
of brine and midday sun.

-- Whom do you seek?
The woman at the centre of the starfish-wheel asks me.
-- I am after another life.

Peter Boyle

There and Then

Friends in a field, their shadows running long into the untilled
ground, and I'm busy trying to catch up, calling for them to
hold on a moment, the voice unfamiliar and the words not my
own, and when I wake I realize the last thing I called to them
might have been the name of the town we were all looking for,
but now it's a summer morning, the light coming in urgent with
day, sheets strewn at the end of the bed, and by the time my
mind reaches out for it, that name or word or thought, it's gone,
perhaps lying there up ahead, with them in the town beyond
the old shed at the edge of the field, with its collection of
discarded tools, hoes and picks and shovels still caked in loam
and soil, the old two-furrow plough and an empty feedbag.
There's a persimmon tree, with its thin covering of leaves and
its branches weighed by tightly packed, hard orange orbs, dense
and ripening, and a thicket of rosemary sprawling about in
the autumn sun, gone wild, looking like it might take over the
world with its thick rough tines, the heavy scent that rubs off
onto skin and lasts all day even after you wake. But thinking of
that town my friends have gone on to, looking out the window
at the summer light, the raging open blue of the sky outside,
I cross past the old shed to where the harrowed ground forms
the first hint of a path between the cherry trees lining the field,
to where a pair of jackdaws come in from the north, creamy
white throats quiet as the flat slate sky above, flit between some
memory of spring, the one gone or the one up ahead.

Michael Brennan

Waiting on Imran Khan

I knew they were trouble the moment they walked in.
I was eighteen, bookish, I'd not yet learned
to build a public face. I was laid open like an oyster
on a salted plate. The uniform was no help,
nylon trousers cut into my soft waist and thighs,
standard issue, there was no bigger size. Summer – the dozy

lunch time shift. Office workers, pensioner couples
sharing, before the cool waterhole of the cinema.
Then, eight or nine men all preening, careening,
igniting against each other. Who was the roughest,
who had the biggest, who was alpha,
and who was his bitch. With my greeting (guinea pig

tentative, I kick myself now), I became the pitch
for a practice hit; a boy's own way to rejig
the middle order of the Pakistani cricket team.
I'd never admired Imran Khan as a cricketer –
too cool and vain – I preferred flashy and passionate
like Dennis Lillee, or stately and dignified

like Clive Lloyd, but even so, it should have been
a thrill. I'd been following the Test series,
a fan since Dad and I sat on The Hill.
For a young man they might have been jovial,
but when I seated them they broke into a dirty laugh,
staring hard at parts of me. I delivered their tray of Pepsi,

my hands shaking so the glasses sang like bells;
not one of them took pity. Imran Khan sat
at the centre. He said something I did not understand
and some of them hooted, one snarled, their eyes

were hot monsters, some swearing softly,
gesturing at me. I met his eye for a long moment

and saw carefully manicured disgust
at the humiliation I was heaping upon myself
by being a young woman, by walking the floor
in my awful uniform, my flat, black lace-up shoes. Yes,
I was walking the floor: earning my own money, slowly
forming the dense quartz of my opinions, polished and patient.

Lisa Brockwell

The Pig

Who would write of a pig
and what would a pig know of Spirit?

Who would think that the soul of a pig,
as it leaves the pig's body,
would create the slightest disturbance in air?

What would a pig know of agony?

What would a pig know of death?

The screaming of a pig
that shreds the air above a village
is no more than the sound
a heavy metal table makes
as it is dragged across stone.

The motionlessness
of a mother in a sow stall
is no more than a pig at rest

the groaning
only the closing of a metal door
far off inside her.

David Brooks

Siren

We walk past the ruined past
pasted to the Academy's cloister walls,
past broken Latin stones' fractured inscriptions,
one fragment reading 'OVE IS',
and I know that though the sea is coming
and volcanoes are not finished with us,
crossing this garden in this courtyard in the evening
with a sentry in a box by the iron gate
watching black-masked fundamentalist
speeches on a laptop on his desk,
all seems to be falling into place
    temporarily and beautifully.

You say goodbye, we say goodbye,
and we drift away down a hillside
past a bar where young people under awnings
drink and talk into the evening, seeming
to know how to live deep into this night,
how to make the harmless sounds of conversation.
We want to sit here too with them on the hillside,
a scooter waiting outside
and an unearthed monstrous stone foot or hand
propped artfully somewhere nearby.

The bluestone cobbles tire our feet as we go down
to a tram where more people out of the night
talk, drink, lean a cheek on the black window glass
of the swinging electric lozenge whose brakes hiss.

As a child I was impatient for night to come properly down,
as if doubt infected the universe as long as dusk lingered.
Doubt was the rope that tied hands behind backs.

Doubt was the door left half open.
Doubt would keep you from the confessional.
I dragged blankets over my head
and my body in soft napped cotton pyjamas
as night at last came down over me neatly.
I wanted it there, then I wanted it gone
when I opened my eyes.

Night, larger than any cathedral, larger than our suburb,
was the thing squatting over us more ancient than childhood,
always interested only in itself.

Tomorrow the sky will reveal a smog-grey streak
swiped across the distant mountains.
We will walk to the top of a nearby hill.
I will remember your legs over me in the night,
your shoulder against mine,
bodies we cannot untangle, their unreadable parts,
Gullivers to the ropes and threads of the night.

We will walk to the top of a nearby hill
and remember something
as the hill falls away below a low wall
all the way down to a river that rolls like a prisoner
in its narrow cell until its mouth spits out the broken
vowels and letters of the past in unheard howls to the sea.

This night in the Academy's cloister
we passed a beautiful stone coffin,
the sliced off tops of columns,
a cocktail party under arches,

and we feel right, we are right,
we step out into the night
and drift down the hillside past a bar

where people sit in semi-dark talking
of the life they have or might have,
glancing up at us as we walk among them,
the night perfect, us perfect too.

The sea is moving, insistent
and volcanoes are considering
what sounds they might now make.
The enormous ruins are held down
and scraped back by bony hands.

The sirens we will hear tomorrow
from the park where we walk
will never cease, they will go round and round
sweeping up whatever they can in their path.

Kevin Brophy

Suspended Belief

'What emerges from urban pixelation is the greyest
of mysteries, furtive glance down an original sidestreet.'
                              (James Stuart, 'Guangdong Sidewalk')

(vision in a Guangzhou wet market)
Discontinuous schedule:
your skeuomorphic watch relics itself,
winds back nothing
weaponises everything.
Live chickens calling from cages
like a chorus in a tragedy.
Your great grandmother's cleaver wiped clean
after cutting a neck in her apartment kitchen.

(curriculum vitae)
Banyan trees with limbs
crosshatching whole apartment blocks,
the sky's sketched edges
rapidly darkening,
and a day already
performance reviewing itself,
with birds retrospectively true
just perching there in point form.

(spring meditation on Du Fu's autumn meditation number eight)
Two immortal companions share a Mercedes
as evening approaches Shanghai.
And when their vehicle passes Yuyuan gardens
shadows float over rebuilt walls
causing vendors look up with concern.
Surely you sense these two even now, don't you,

when the lights on Weihai road flicker?
Stay calm. Predict a surplus. Everything is gain.

(Deutero-systematic perception)
At a traffic crossing
in the French concession
a peripheral injunction arrives,
spirit-whispered like the oral law.
But you can only half-hear it
over the world's constant notifications,
those angel-servants delivering winds
when trucks flash past.

(incarnate suburb)
The quarried stone body of the city
is not your body, for the paths
of Beijing's citizens are beyond
tracing out. You remember
being younger, learning about China
from a returned church missionary,
copying his measured facts onto a piece of white
cardboard, reading the country back into yourself.

Lachlan Brown

Rooibos

the day goes by

all day it's a bit later
                than it should be

by late afternoon
        there's less than an hour
    to wring
            colour
        from the backyard sky

            ~

crouching in to the internet
            to counter
                    intensity,
lassitude does work
                eventually

            ~

        is it ok,   in a deflated poem
to just keep everything
                    on the surface,
be abstruse?

                    for instance -
    scraping a page of coal
                into an imitation hybrid

like an open cut simile

              the section
                      that could change everything
the way
       some chance concatenation
                                    can

          plus there's always
              'the things it'll do
              not to be a sonnet'

          ~

stumbling
        on spongy wetpoured rubber
                    fig litter fake footpath
              under the long limb of the tree
         big fig on Ocean Street

      a moment's notice

   passing Johann Wolfgang von Goethe's
institut
      is it full of maxims?

          sensor light tripped

Jupiter
        slowly moving
                    towards Venus
        as we turn
a space station
            ascends between them

little Pluto's due soon
        close,   not close enough to see

these things
        seem   what?
    wondrous?

& the less wondrous stuff
        rocket parts
              collision fragments
defunct satellites   debris crap
                    orbiting
        a spaced out graveyard?

on earth   an irregular line -
        bulky polymer bins'
      angles gleaming
    the lane's dark sentinels

in the convolvulus
        a wet stick spider
    protects its sac
                of spiderlings

                ~

up early, quiet
        at the stove
                brewing rooibos

it's spitting outside,
    remember
                'devils' tears'
sunlight's shower of rain
                by the freezing Spree

a post-wall anniversary
'Happy Birthday Burger King'
   was possibly
           the last sentence
you ever said to me
      there
    near Lichtenberg,
         on Frankfurter Allee

your style of joke

          now
           worn thin

    ~

making sure
   the grill door's slid to
 & locked

driving southwest
  in a borrowed car
     ignoring
warning beeps
     & the dashboard's
  little blinking light

buildings stuck
  around
the airport tunnel exhaust stacks

blood & fur
  squashed brushtail possum
    on the M5

show me
> a marsplu
> a marsuple
> a marsupial
>> no one likes

~

so,
> what is
>> 'cool jazz'?

~

disconsolate today

it's like
> my hand is
>> planted
> next to
the mexican marigold
> & is going to grow there

~

a hyperactive sparrow
> flits in for seed

~

> can't get up

imagine
> tunnelling to java

~

like to keep
        some mistakes in,
  like a drip
        in a monochrome painting

Pam Brown

bound

a small book with a varnished
wood cover bound with leather
flowers <u>from</u> the holy land inscribed
to my mother from a friend in the armed
forces *bill, jerusalem 1941   flowers and*
views <u>of</u> the holy land   it says inside   in three
languages   hebrew english french   each of twelve
oblongs of card has a sprig of pressed flowers glued
to its back   twelve hand tinted images of various
iconic scenes: deep and rich as illuminated dreams;
the flowers' colours have faded   the tissue interlaid
turned brown   but mostly the shapes of the tiny leaf
sprigs are firm and resolute; one flower has lost its
leaf and stalk but its red petals reveal a patient
heart   the vanished stalk has left a pale
imprint   it endures, this tenacious ghost —
as a three year old i visited bill's rose bay home
in a block of flats in balfour road   a name that
matters   like allenby street in the picture of old
tel-aviv   underneath the main inscription he had
written, now in purple ink *more & more & still more -*
of all you wish yourself   i'm trying to keep this
poem simple just 'flowers from the holy land' like
an intact reverie   but this old gift of a book leans
unprotected never gathering dust on a poetry shelf
two down - i suddenly note - from 'selected
poems of darwish', born 1941, galilee
where did his 'carnations' grow ~

Joanne Burns

* The *carnations* image comes from a Mahmoud Darwish poem
I Have Witnessed the Massacre

Car Lover

It can be healing to walk the vacant streets
of these suburbs, over tree-buckled pavements,
the ground cicatrised, I'm a proverb of missing
woman with tablet, with handbag evidence.

It can be therapy to loiter in the park, streetlamps
glow with yellow discernments though V8 utes
may be scarce, the road rule is swift and strobic.
The sky is gagged but I'm a sentence in heels.

Trees camber, pencilled in mist, row by row.
Cars gear in/out of driveways front or rear-ended
with gear-stick discovery. A frogmouth cautions me,
the rose-lit church grounds pray for my flesh.

Consider me slumped cold against a brick wall.
What device pedals thought's accessories?
Cars sing hosannas for the freeway, pulsing
nocturnal. I improvise, I turn like leaves rasping.

Dumped by sleep's apparatus, there is a girl who
beckons from below the liquidambar. I've heard
her chafing. Bring an ice pick. Send a coupé to
abduct me, my bones whistle of that other Spring.

Michelle Cahill

Cloaca Maxima

Any, every, thing that was exposed
goes underground and is washed into the Tiber.
This is what some people do

with faces, burying. You see them,
the heavy ones, chests like rivers, their heads
bowed down with great

antlers of thought invisible.
After many seasons, the fronts of their bodies
terribly developed to carry them.

Venus of the Drains, the woman with the scum
at the corners of her mouth who talked
for a long time, scarred by burning, perilous thin,

then told us we had made her day.
It is seen, what should not be seen. It is I sees it.
Shameful, to feel so heavily the shame

of others—to hear and echo
that note always waiting in the voice to be sung.
Do I make it happen

to her by having

face and chest that wash with red?

Elizabeth Campbell

Axe derby

Never were knuckle-men.
Choked up on planks

of smoke, they haul
towards the peplum, stabbing

back at time, splinters of it
flip like cars. Rolled sleeves,

knees cooked, the rousie
is flirting with her broom, a blonde

with criminal simplicity with
historical truth we can detoxify

a poisoned planet. Now
they're descending the spirit heap

dribbling pinkies along fair knotty thighs.
Children are returning to pick up the butts.

Still the brunette is caving in the face
of time, is making herself a living

treasure from this surplus
hour the minutes fly

Bonny Cassidy

Plan B

After Vivienne Plumb, 'The alternative plan'

Plan A: find man sympathetic to children but who loves me best of all. *Plan B*: become pregnant. *Plan C*: surf web re older mothers & childbirth. *Plan D*: establish relationship, difficult enough without a child. *Plan E*: buy lingerie, stay single & childfree. *Plan F*: push borrowed labradoodle pup around block in borrowed $1,200 pram. *Plan G*: stay single & have baby that doesn't bite. *Plan H*: search web for sperm donor without tatts. *Plan I*: have one-night stand with only gym bloke not on steroids. *Plan J*: prick condoms with sterile needle. *Plan K*: second-night stand with same gym bloke (despite 'roids). *Plan L*: separate finding partner from acquiring child. *Plan M*: search web re twins by artificial insemination. *Plan N*: time travel to fifteenth-century Florentine orphanage with Kathmandu carry pack. *Plan O*: move to Italy, *this plan requires* proficiency in Italian & a grant. *Plan P*: *think of another plan*. *Plan Q*: search web re overseas adoption agencies with sympathetic international agreements (*finance dependent*). *Plan R*: arrange wealthy patron, superior sperm & gravy baster without telling therapist. *Plan S*: observe o/s adoptees' picnic in skanky suburb. *Plan T*: terminate contact with sperm donor & surrogate agencies. *Plan U*: visit a single mum's chat room disguised as Leila the foetus. *Plan V*: join kidnapping chat room. *Plan W*: become novice in Our Lady Queen of Procreation Convent. *Plan X*: pray for visitation from male angel with no active addictions & grand sperm count. *Plan Y*: Search web re Renaissance names. *Plan Z*: *Change nothing*.

Julie Chevalier

Magnolia

A son's birth means tragedy now.
                        'Song of the War-Carts', Du Fu

I rise from my pallet: it is still dark
and the men are asleep, their naked chests
inflating and collapsing like a smith's bellows.

The moon hangs beneath the clouds: soon
autumn will arrive, winds rippling the fields.
Back in my village, the farmers are preparing

for the harvest. I press together strips of linen,
line it with moss I'd picked from the base of trees.
It is my time, and my secret. Tomorrow we advance

towards the border. The war-carts are loaded,
the horses will be tethered to their burdens.
Here the quivers of arrows wait to be spent.

I carry a skin of water and squat in the grasses.
Now it is safe to loosen my robes. Carefully, I clean myself.
Even in the dark, my hands are sticky with blood.

***

My first kill was a chicken. It was the new year.
Father handed me his knife and gestured at our hen.
She strutted around the yard, cocking her head this way

then that, scratching and searching for worms.
In the bamboo coop her brood of chicks cried warning.
I pushed up my sleeves and advanced. No fear –

we'd done this before, her and I. This was betrayal.
I carried her to the back of the hut, her heartbeat
pulsing in my palm. Her feathers so alive against my skin.

***

My faithful horse bears me for many miles, carries me
into battle, comforts me with his touch. Between my legs,
the saddle creaks my name: *Mu Lan, Mu Lan.*

Not for me the embroidered magnolias of marriage;
I give birth to nothing but blades, arrows and death.
My sword is my husband, my brothers my men.

They think me one of them. I drink sweet wine
fermented from plums; I curse and spit and plot.
I kill without mercy. Beneath my armour, secreted

in a pouch: a carved jade favour from the King.
In the night I draw my fingers across the dragon
twisting around the sun. The morning dawns emerald.

***

A soldier unfurls a banner and I plant it deep
in the soil. Another day, another frontier.
Men are busy at the fires: they grind millet

and cook it into gruel. So many mouths to feed,
so many sons, fathers, brothers... How much longer
before I gaze upon the lined face of my own father?

Beyond us, the mountains rise in mockery.
Wei is surrounded, corralled on all sides:
Qin, Zhao, Yan, Qi, Chu, Han...

If I were a hawk I would take off, wing towards
the west and the setting sun. I would hunt only
to survive, I would feather a nest, I would fly.

Eileen Chong

Notes:
The poem is based on a legendary character in Chinese history, Hua Mu Lan.
This character was first recorded in *The Ballad of Mulan*, a work thought to
have been transcribed around the 6th century A.D. in *Musical Records of Old
and New*. While the original text has been lost, the tale has survived in an 11th
century anthology, the *Music Bureau Collection*, which clearly attributes the
source of the text.

Hua Mu Lan was a young woman who dressed as a man in order to take her
father's place in battle. She rose to become a General during the Northern
Wei dynasty (386–536 ad). It is said that she served in battle for a total of
twelve years before returning to her village.

I have taken poetic license with the use of the seven Warring States, which
were in existence during the Zhou dynasty (1046–256 bc) and not during the
Northern Wei dynasty.

Secondary

Angling over star-fields, the pitches
lit like billiard tables.
Those lengths you were shouted up
and back, lungs scoured
by Brillo air. The lazier concord
of close mown grass and low hanging fruit
of the short boundary. A tang
of primitive electronics: the circuit board's
braille labyrinth, the slab type
of Amstrad. This callow path you cannot take
curves around and through
the way a perfect river might. You find
a little gate unlatched,
and the light tangles, as you step
into the ferment: into the heady reek of itch.

The aubergine, by the window, glossy
as an eight ball: lavender,
the road, a torn-open
mountain pouring cloud. Noble erosions
from sceptre to cushions,
from mitre to trademark. A lavish
glut of adjectives, dissolving
in a merlot hour – flabby as any
soft landing among
the rubber bells of foxgloves.
The heart as wound or badge, a tattoo
smudged like junk-mail wet.
A fading haze from clubs
like grates where fires have been –
signs hung out as dirty washing.

Easier to paint
than rhyme, this volatility. A poet-envy
of the art-fluke, or ripeness
cut in segments sucked to the pith.
A plaintive case deflating
on a snack bar counter
where citrus men
swash fizz through lunch
and later repair the voltage of night
in the out-of-sync bounce
of signal and blinker.
You take a little kindling, the light
of a cupped match,
to hazard across deciduous campuses:
the vast, blue continent of theory. Go, softly on.

Aidan Coleman

Hinterland

first the   mag
nificent stone   slapped
                         across the valley
                  /

(acacia brushing the gusts

leaking with shadow, the dark glows
asking the pastures), then
                      to play
                   /
              my turn
      to balance on a thermal, dizzy
                    with eagle
   rivulets of vineyards and scattered avocado

                      groves
        glints in an eye, a single, I'm joining
            \
                 with the split, gulps
         at a sun, itdoeswhatitdoes, painting
               the etceteras
                    — of topoi
            the vast plumes of broccoli
   the heads of the innumerable gums
     \
        stooping to draw the path
              the canopy's hazy scales

                   the cusp of
       weight, fluvial wake coiled tight
        around solemn magnets, they

                              mash paints, all that brush
                                                    \ \

                        from here to the image of it
                      from the light to what leads it
                   the burning eye of a snake coiling
))
into the west   I can see its path   I can sense
                                what it might do as I step

                out
and fill my intention
                        with curling canyon
)
strings of creeks r
                  attling b
                              ack to the coast

Stuart Cooke

ABOVE US

Above us we hear the windmill yelping, circling like a
trapped dog while the house sits like a black skull on the
hill. Above us the tombs are rising from their rest and
travelling along the roads beneath trees turning sourly.
Above us the wind flings uncountable seed into the
dignified light tossed through the depths by a green moon
rolling over and over in the shifting lens of the waves.
Above us nakedness stretches forever against danger,
ravishment and smoke. When we wake our lives are on fire.
Above us only our sleepy souls drifting like reeds catching the air.

MTC Cronin

Swimming (my lane)

The bug is in my lane, drowning fast,
riding the ripples I make, picking at the water
with hopeless oars, frantically gathering loss.
My times are slipping but I still have reasons
for getting wet every day, hauling myself
up that long, black line, the monologue
I have to follow. The print keeps me straight,
a fat stemmed gift I steer to a sudden T.
I've seen so many—junctions, crossroads—
relapsing every twenty-five metres. All I do
is cry out, kick off, go back like moving forward,
up and down that stem, flushed by routine,
the reach and rob of constructive habit.
So I scoop the bug in the pool of my palms.
I don't think of Anne Sexton right away.
It's later I recall her posthumous title,
The Awful Rowing Toward God. Over again,
keeping the beat upon waves of my own
making, wrestling at daybreak above
tissues of light that shed with every stroke
I'm attempting. Holding the course, rowing
the surface, working these bags of breath.
I scooped the bug just to cup my hands
as in the days when I had faith to receive.

Nathan Curnow

Heisenberg Saying Goodbye
to Mum at Lilyfield

Every construction is temporary, including the fire altar.
                                        Roberto Calasso

Accommodate the action in your life
to wrest the deep perspective of the real
from cubic content realms of atmosphere
at play beyond the bank and shoal of time.

Then resonance begins, and all vibrates.
The syntax of position no more sculpts
this world of interpenetrative forms
than syntaxes of motion render grace.

Yet syntax is the caul on all our births;
and mothers claw the membrane from our eyes
to fret us into life, in losing theirs.
From there, each choice engraves a different choice.

The decades pass. One needle for one groove.
The canticles flare chaos from the spin.
The gyre to crackly zero stays the same.
(You've got to love the Hindus more than most.)

We saw grand sweeps of swells from tiny arcs.
We sliced the wave face, tumbling into light.
My mother hugged me goodbye at seventy-three,
knowing, just then, her strength may outlive mine.

Accommodate the action in your life,
she said, to aeronautical exhausts
of every plane and cab I ever caught
(my own arcs more elaborate than most).

Accommodate the action of your life,
she seemed to say: make past and future fuse.
I felt her fingers dig into my back:
That strength I had is yours. Things die. Not love.

Luke Davies

Wooden Horse

on your crude wooden sled,
you were once –
a broom, a length of rope,
a handful of off-cuts,
two screws and eight
three inch nails.
You are not quite symmetrical:
one rocker pine,
the other, hardwood.
And your plank torso has
more of a bevel on the left
than the right.
Your hard round eye
has been drilled right through
your plank face;
from above
this gives you a bright
dark vacancy.
To a child this might lend
perspicacity (squatting
and peering I can see
the evening ocean through
your clear gaze);
the same bit bore
the hole for the dowel handle
that impales your jaw;
your profile is not equine,
more Border Leicester.
Someone also drilled three holes
at your rear and four
at the back of your head
inserting and gluing

the cut frayed rope.
But your crimped tail
and mane were tufts of stubble
like nibbled wallaby grass
when you first came our way.
Your broom legs are so straight,
slender as a racehorse's.
I forgot to say
that there is some pathos
about your routered mouth
and its odd slope of forbearance.
Your broom neck leans forward
towards the future.
I suspect you never boasted
a coat of paint; nowadays
you are so weathered you
might be made of driftwood –
a horse of the sea.
Your balance is exact,
the elipse of each crude arc
rocker knows to baulk
just before the tipping point.
Earless, eyeless yet not blind,
bereft of mane and tail
you are steadfast, gazing
through that vacancy
to east and west,
seeing not, in your long life,
that children grow old,
but how, from each tide,
rolls the continuum of each wave.

Sarah Day

Following the many elbows of the Yarra

Following the many elbows of the Yarra.
        Taking the racing line.
Retracing the route to the Toorak school that
did not teach, but bequeathed a tie.
Perhaps, I was blinded
by the nostalgia of a life half lived,
perhaps, and did not see
the vixen spirit herself across the road
just in time to feel the bite of my tyres.
There was no time to brake.
My foot was half on,
        half off, the accelerator
when I felt the shock of her through
my steering wheel, heard her cry.
I could have kept driving into the night—
the road was dead, the streets asleep—
but could not forget that time when,
coming down Brown Mountain in a Toyota,
I killed a goanna and kept going,
        lacked the decency
to drag her carcass off the road,
and how I carried that sin
in my glove compartment still.
I stopped. Stepped out into the early morning,
the air cold enough to turn breathe to steam,
and stood by the taillights of my old 318,
watched the fox lie in the glare of a street light,
half a world away from her natural home,
        and felt something close to pity.
Waited until a fleeting shadow
        —at first an eclipse—
grew smaller, darker, then manifested
as a wedge-tailed eagle that landed

on the double-white line without a sound,
wing tips sweeping the leaves
from the blue-black road.
                The eagle was telling me
she was watching me
                watch the fox.
So, now I knew I had no choice.
I had to act. I left my car behind,
purring its soft red cloud of carcinogens,
and heard my boots strike the bitumen
as I drew close enough to see my animus
reflected in her animal eye.
The vixen was breathing
                —more like panting—
and unable to move more than her head.
Without thinking, I reached down
to touch her burnt orange fur,
but she had seen enough of my kind
on her backyard travels
and, throwing her head up, caught
my thumb in the trap of her razor teeth.
What happened next surprised us all.
Without speaking,
                I took off my old school tie
to bind my bleeding hand,
walked back to the car,
                popped the boot and came
back to the fox with the wheel jack
swinging low from my good hand,
then let that hand rise and fall
beneath the shadow of the street light,
and listened to the sound
                of steel splintering bone
while the eagle lifted herself from the road
to seek solace in the sky.

Joel Deane

The Silence of Siskins

For my grandfather

He circles my arrival
on the calendar.

It is late November
and it doesn't snow.

A wooden pallet
hardens his bed.

He dreams of grandmother.
He doesn't want new dreams.

Two siskins in cages —
their song frozen like the air

that other November
when she lost her heart

cleaning and baking
for those who might arrive.

Above the fireplace a few flies
are nervous company.

'Not easy on earth,' he says,
'not easy below.'

Jelena Dinic

untitled: villaknelle xvi

I think it's awfully dangerous to give general advice
to those dying of drink or shipwreck, suicide, one thing or
another
once you know how to observe them, it's wise

not to try to form people in your own image: fancy old
fashioned boom boom, cloak-and-dagger Georgian scenes,
I think

it's awfully dangerous to give general advice
as one gets older one cannot distinguish genius
among new, younger men ('purchase woollen underwear
because of the damp stone')
once you know how to observe them, it's wise to

visit the dead in their triangular sitting rooms
wives typing forgotten names that no longer exist
I think it's awfully dangerous to give general advice

to revolutionaries weeping over a cat that's gone wrong
a force without it's limitations, once
you know how to observe them, it's wise to violate

the laughing sources, common as speech, essential and permanent
and gloomy indeed, I think
it's awfully dangerous to give general advice
once you know how to observe them, it's wise to
violate rules

Paris Review, Spring-Summer 1959, #21 (T.S. Eliot)

Dan Disney

Right Through Me

Little mortal,
afraid of all the sounds that
see into my body, afraid
of the techo's patient gaze
at the big screen where
Mr Muerto might be playing.
When they pin me to the plasma
the bony bit of me in tiny
with one perfect stone, is it,
or knot from some ancient accident?
Can you remember any trauma?
they ask, and I want to say
childhood falls from trees,
delirious, just because you could,
and being pulled roughly back
from dreaming on the Capri funicular.
But I just shrug
and feel the rightness
of withholding these lived jolts that
go right through me.

Lucy Dougan

A northern winter

For Ken Bolton (who found it)

1

bitter gall in afternoon light
stroboscopic beech
'we will shortly be arriving at / Rainham'

a stationmaster spits the whistle

Tate Modern: Delaunay (Robert) and Severini, Munch and
Bonnard, Jonas Mekas' films. Gerhard Richter.

Before me (from the members' room), St Pauls and the
Millenium Bridge. I will walk that way towards Lamb's Conduit
(via Shoe Lane, Holborn and Red Lion Streets), for Peter Riley
and Peter Philpott at The Lamb.

a glass, seemingly of port, at the window of The Dolphin
(this sad enterprise of notation)

2

Today I sit downstairs in the office, looking out the back
window to our garage and wall and, above it, the last few yellow
leaves against a (rare) blue sky.

I see the sage plant beneath the window and immediately smell
(purely imaginary) sage.

3

What troubles me about Jackson MacLow's methods is the mere
thought of method. It seems essential that these works enunciate
their principles of construction i.e. primary text, letter selection
and secondary text. But is the knowledge of this supposed to
bolster our appreciation of the result? If so are we admiring it
because it fills the brief or are we admiring it for what it is? The
two things are not necessarily compatible. MacLow realised at a
certain point that there was no such thing as the purely aleatory,
that the first principles were already an aesthetic decision.

4 (Three musical interludes)

i

Charlie Watts, dapper in Hatchards bookshop
a South London accent that may have been worked on

ii

in my head, the Horrie Dargie Quintet play
'East of the Sun and West of the Moon'

iii

I'd always hated Gary Shearston singing 'I get a kick out of
you', but suddenly in the student bar, Roehampton, it all,
especially the violinist, sounds good.

5

The snow from two nights back hasn't melted. Interesting to
see which plants seem to have survived – lavender, thyme,
oregano – that you might have expected to wilt. Tarragon dies
off naturally, the rosemary hasn't really got going.

6

A white oblong of sun on the bedroom wall

Tonight, a reading in London which I'm not going to. That's three London events I'll have missed this week. Two because of weather, one, inertia.

7

nothing in this drawer

a tangle of script

'snowbound'

I feel less 'at home' here than I did a year ago. But would I feel 'at home' anywhere else?

8

If I have always envisaged work as music why do I still fear abandoning a patina of sense? The poems on the surface are 'documentary', but documents themselves don't 'last'. We don't read the poets (for the most part) for insights into the contemporary (though they ignore the past at their own peril).

9

speckled lights from Christmas
fake chandeliers

out there it's winter still
the bulbs in public gardens unopened

I decided today, walking through Canterbury, that what I feel now is a kind of blankness, a nothingness which seems neither bad nor good, neither exhilarating nor terrifying. It is maybe 'despond'. I need to emerge from it to write again, or if I write again I will emerge from it. I'm not certain which of these is true.

Now, I suppose, is the moment I stop being an observant tourist and become an ignorant local. Yet at the same time Australia appears an even odder construction. I mean I love it, aspects of it at least, but from here it's a peculiar thing. The fires that I know much about make it to the UK news, as does (as ever) 'shark attack'.

I belong to a space that nobody here will recognise.

10

spring bitter
and bitter spring
at The Sun

shadows on a page, the rise and fall of breath
striations in an enormous fireplace

marking time
marking, re-
marking

'Jim Thompson
never materialised
again'

11

The Fitzroy Tavern, Charlotte Street, last seen in, was it, 1992 or 1987? The 'writers and artists' bar is downstairs, but I stay

up, 'not writing', trying to remember the name of the Italian
restaurant I'm supposed to be at in half an hour.

telephones that ring like telephones

the ghost of Julian Maclaren-Ross shuffles past

'a violent hash smoker shakes a chocolate machine'

12

teasel
the burr of the plant, dried,
a device for carding wool

leaves that jump (dead ones) with a sound like raindrops
small greenish birds
an orange butterfly (fritillary?)

now I know the yew, found in churchyards, is poison to livestock

13

and now it's daylight saving

when will the scaffolding come down?

and what place for *this* scaffold
in the age of interruption?

miniature daffodils under the tarpaulin
a sign ('The Sun') on its side;
inside, from the rafters,
hops, still green from summer

Laurie Duggan

Black Deaths in Custody

despite the cost a new gaol has been built
it seems the incarceration rates are trebling
I only came here in the role
of a Deaths In Custody inspector
all the cells are stark and spotless
blank screens watch from the corner
the offices have the highest technology
the faces of the staff still look the same

when I walk down this wing and peer
into this filthy room the door closes behind me
the feeling in my heart is changing
from a proud strength of duty to fear
all the stories I have ever heard
stand silent in the space beside me—
a coil of rope is being pushed
under the door of this cell

Ali Cobby Eckermann

Hearts and Minds

What was that horror film with Peter Lorre?
The man who'd lost his hands,
On whom the hands of a dead murderer
Were grafted (gruesome story)
And rapidly proceeded to transfer
To him the killer's murderous commands.

And yet it's said of heart transplants that patients
Inherit from their donors
More than that vital muscle. They present,
It's said, strange alterations
Of predilection, mood and temperament
(Changes of heart) known to those foregone owners.

The heart, to the Egyptians, was the seat
Of mind, intelligence.
But did they really, locked in silent thought,
And feeling the heart beat,
Sense consciousness behind the sternum, caught
In a cage of ribs, watching, as it invents,

All this? Can we be sure it beats behind
The sockets of our eyes,
The hand-propped forehead, one inseparable
Hybrid of brain and mind
Autonomously humming in the skull?
Too dizzying a crux to analyse.

What if, no neural spectre we possess
And call on to reprise
The fictions of the self in which it's pent,
It washes bodiless
Around us like a primal element,
Like weather blowing through the open trees.

Stephen Edgar

working from home – to do list

12 buttons brown thread
take your psyche for a walk
pack the wheelchair
into the station wagon
for the doctor's
kiss the cat
kiss the cat?
the cat died years ago
water the herbs
pray over the olive tree
drench your yesterdays in salt water
mend your mother's trousers
get the sewing machine serviced
forgive someone something
try to remember what it was
cook tea tonight
it's your turn
get the washing off the line
before it rains
make another list
fill the thesaurus
check the oil and water
in the dictionary
find a page of tomatoes
in the fruit bowl
stack the bookshelves with rice
dust the wattle
water the nouns and verbs
prune the adjectives and adverbial clauses
write a downpipe print a seedling
phone a friend
take yourself out and shake

the crumbs onto the grass
listen to mozart or the clash
bpay something
narrate a tree or a mote of dust
eat hopkins drink leonard cohen
smell the first leaves of your next book
brew them in your best pot
haiku your neighbour's cat
finish your new cardigan
put teardrops into a dry eye
leave nothing out
and everything in the rain
including yourself
writing

Anne Elvey

Death of a Year

Our memories of ruin fail to make it through customs. The
helicopters rave, make no sense; somehow they know what
      they're doing
But go back, thoughts, to laughter and neurotic running around
a European city. An exchange of books through a third
party. There is one friend in these cases that takes on a huge
debt. The newspaper columns write themselves, they are writers
      of a generation, they
were implicated in the mistakes that everyone made. To not
enforce them in an obit would itself be betrayal. White
spaces indicate hospital, erect letters represent love. We were
way too tired to think of going on with
life as it was. There was no room for projects of small ambition
of mere example. The appropriate would go on being perpetrated
      but not by
us. In the Slovene city, the tea house drips with rust from
the local trees. The trace of poetry in the air only with
the mention of the dead's name. It was a year of change here
too. A white sea eagle in a too small tree foretold of knowledge
disappearing; a blue-faced honeyeater would forever be our
bird of mourning. The surety of a line paired
with the thrusting of translation; unlabelled orange juice
I'm drunk. Perhaps we still have grave dirt on our hands
      The city rumbles
This close to the centre, the lights never go out, lovers and
starers-into-rivers mean the bridges are never clear. As our
      friends
knew, a lot of loss can inhere in a year. A whole town can
be wiped out. A habitat, a type of mole or fly. We have their
recorded voices of course. We can turn our backs on what
we have and let it disappear like we're asleep. In our
dreams we're being hunted in a forest that is itself endangered

We're passengers in a car, joking at each enjambment we
survive

Michael Farrell

Requiem

a sock falls from the line
like the market
responding to rumours of Grexit
& it strikes him surprising
that death makes the imagined real
   in the old-fashioned way.

an expected text
still changes the direction of things,
the way every discarded beer bottle
submerged in sediment
   readjusts the river's current.

when we go beyond the clouds
we feel the collapse of dreams more keenly
   & even if all there was to lose
was lost some time ago

and it is the scope of that which wasn't
that clumsily cleaves the heart
like a jihadi's dull blade through
an aid worker's pale neck.

Liam Ferney

Janus

DAMMED CHI

RAIN COLLECTS LIBELLOUS NOISE
ABOVE THE MASSES THE STORM
AN OBSCURED MIRROR OF THE TOXIC BE
RIVERS & CHILDISH LORDS
LOW THERE'S ALWAYS SOME
DAMMED CHI SOMEWHERE
IN THE WORLD WE BREATHE IN
THE CARBON PLAGUE OF SUBURBIA
CORPSE ORATIONS & THEIR TURF
WARS MIND YOU THE WORLD HAS NO
HEAD OR SPIRIT IT OCCUPIES ITSELF
W/ SCIENCE NOT SEANCE HOMELESS
ITS MEMORIES ARE RHYTHMIC
CALCULUS FALLING FROM THE SKY

SUNNET

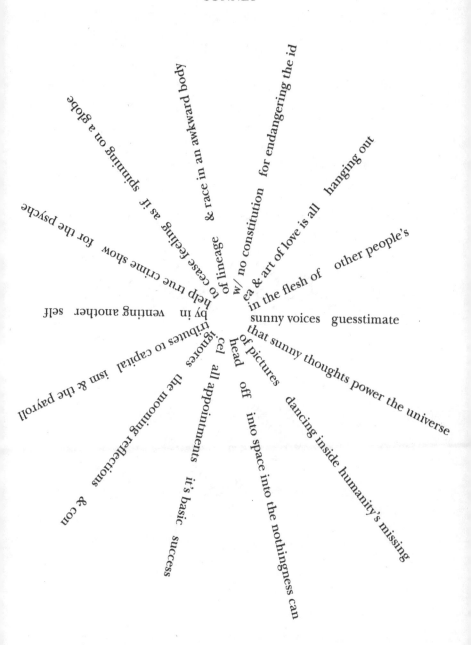

VINTAGE

THE NOUVEAU WILL SOON BE FACT
CHECKED HUNTED OUT IN THE AIR
SUMMER NOCTURNAL DEAD FLOWERS
KNOCK KNOCK A QUAINT CHORUS OF
FORM A QUAINT CHORUS OF THOSE
VOICES LOOKING TO BAN ENDLESSLY
SELF-DIGITISING TO BAN ENDLESSLY
P R E S T I D I G I T I S I N G
YOUTH WHO DROOL OP O
TIMISTICALLY W/ ADAGIO
S T A L E SOPHISTICATION SPECI
ENCASED AS PHYSICAL EN
MEN SO ANTI & NAIVE
GARDE W/ YOUR REARGUARD

not a zip
of the current
mirrors this world
isn't that what we
want? our creative
juices idle afflicted
with the   beautifully
iffy a mass flu of
d r e a m s / d r o n e s
perfect beings   are
random the move
ment of one's seat
can set off all harm
o n y x   in the   a i r
tho ugh it's optional
being anti & doesn't
MEAN resisting
the fear of collapse
when upping the
ante lickety split
a zealous romp be
proud not prude
childlike

Toby Fitch

Ambition Man

The things us Murri blackfellas have to go over in life's
Futures is hard.
Love's gone bad and less money and work.
This easy going one got the flour tea sugar our mothers and
    fathers worked for.
We were black men before the lot say, Ah ah, what's colour got
    to do with it?
Well the light comes from the dark.
May our babies never forget the black men who washed clean
    and were kind on the began.
The things we men went into were hard but changes were seen.
Now we sit as if space chases around our necks and our hands
    have no arts.
To sell the spirit of the good dance we get nothing in going on.
To let sin overtake our wind wins we will never bow down.
Most Murri today are national
Yes we do know the borders
But our unity is we knew this before they told us.
Ambition black red and gold men come forward now take us
In songs of love and fighter rights.

Lionel G. Fogarty

XXXI

I'd like to write a poem in which guru
was in the first or second line. Then
I'd quote from an Indian sage, pepper
the poetry with references to love,
add a further reference to a spicy affair,
hope the mix was right to salt a wound.
Cinnamon opens the heart. Avoid cumin
if you're in a courting mood. Matchbrokers
know this. A bride must serve papadums
fried in sesame oil if she's to woo a lover.
The bond's snapped, what's left to pick over?
I won't anoint myself with turmeric
or saffron powder. There'll be no garland.
I'll fry some sweets then dip them in syrup.

Tina Giannoukos

from Empirical

V

Now I will walk again into this field of wreckage
which is my starting place—On its stone heaps the tussock
is dry stalks the colour of a scratch in glass and rattling fennel
tendrils from the root—A single cloud
now coming in over the motorway on slow dissolves of light—
Along the cutting's side speargrass with a rain wind in it
moves through the shape of a catching fire—This
stoppedness before rain in which years I have forgotten
invent a landscape still in what I have named landscape—
ruinable, incandescent, piece by piece drawn
into that blank in thought which sets the names
in their array—tussock, speargrass, wild fennel—bright charges
hung upon abyss—Do you remember?
In head-high grass, its pale seedheads, the wind is massing
light, lights moving in place and scattering down—
At the level of my eye the grass untidy, touchable, steeply
its slant stalks narrowing back into their likeness—
A train which even now is sending its long cry back
out of the vanishing point it keeps discovering from the scene—
The rain is first a prickling sound and then hand hair eyes all
touch and does not know me walled in itself, its dazzling blank—
The road will come through here—

Lisa Gorton

The Latter Days

I sit on the porch in darkness
and imagine I have been assigned to watch here on my own.
At 3 o'clock everyone is sleeping,
no distant drone
of a car now, nor bird chirping.
Downhill, there was wiped from the town
the last house-lights, as if they were moisture.
The main street goes on
beyond its lamps, which are pinches of salt, and becomes
    among the landscape
a javelin thrown.

There is an engorged moon
and the coarse-ground stars, and there's one sullen light across
    the valley –
a farmhouse, on its mountain,
beneath the folded plumage of the sky.
The range there
is crumpled, as the blanket is
I have drawn about me. I am reminded by that blood-shot glare
I was tonight in Hades,

or believed so. I went down through a gate in the marshland,
in a reek of sulphur,
and passed below what must have been a lintel,
into thin flavourless metal air.
Then I realized that the souls in Hades
cannot change, since they've been judged,
and I understood, too late, there was no point in seeking
my father's bitter face among the Shades.

Yet I must go on.
It was not for revenge – there is only grief.
Although I have grown old
this is an ageless wound.
The regret is for his chances, all lost in dissipation. That is as
    difficult
as always, and growing older, it would seem,
has served no purpose at all.

I thought I came there through a forest, where the trees
    howled like dogs.
Thick as the leaves of an endless autumn
that I had trod
in the wilderness, on the river bank
were the dead,
swept together, wearied,
who waited for a ferry, which would mean their journey was
    almost ended.
Somehow I stepped across the Stygian water,

and Pluto sat in the plain, as though a crag upreared.
Proserpine lay along his side,
under a pall of steamy darkness.
They were draped in cerements, from their lustreless crowns to
    the ground,
and I could not see her beauty,
for which she was snatched away
while gathering flowers in the meadows of Enna.
The tremulous souls on the bare plains behind her
were more numerous than grass might have been.

Then my father appeared
on a single warp in the atmosphere
(while the hands of the dead fell upon me
in a feeble rain). And of course he was as he must always remain –

he had no guilt, not even feigned,
no greeting for me. As in the nursing home,
I felt him demand, of earth and of the zenith, 'Get me out of here.'
Pitiful spirit,
born of an ill-featured star,
hollowed by thirst, he seemed to say, with all of his old extremity,
'There is no crime
I would not commit
to be born again, and take my chances on earth.'
Young men blame others, and old men themselves, except for
      him.
And his clamour was sealed away
in the human quicksand of the crowd.

For a while, they have their little dreams there
that show them they are sleeping.
But no one can live forever, not even the dead. They will fade.
It is suggested
in Virgil that only a few heroes ever reach
the shimmering light-filled uplands of the blest, Elysium.

Then I found I had got up and was leant against the railing,
to feel on my face the tender
incandescence of the dew.
There was a snarl
of lightning, where it threw itself along the horizon.
I brought a drink out
and saw, in passing, the piled-up cold woodash trickle
in the grate, as when a breeze,
memento mori,
stirs among the feathers of a guinea fowl.

The advantage of having sought an education
was Virgil as companion,
although, of course, he did not condescend

to walk with me. I had for a guide-book
what was made of him by Dryden,
in sufficient accuracy.
I knew what one must do: that in Hades you break off
the candelabra of a bough
from out of a misty tree; each flame
on this becomes gold-leaf, and you carry it before you
onto the wide steps
that lead steeply into darkness, welling from below.
The branch is for Proserpine, an offering,
its small light
to be planted in her shadow, although it will not flourish.

One time, we greeted our father as 'Mr Shellfish',
playing with a remark our mother had made.
He ignored us
except to point out that Horace found abhorrent
any violation of the ordinance of nature
such as was involved in calling him a crab.
He contended that his pension was meant for him,
who'd been infested with TB, while mired on a side-line
of the War. If our mother reminded him that this was self-
    inflicted,
and was exacerbated
continuously, he would retaliate by wounding us
with the porcelain claw
of his disdain.

I associate him always with the Latin authors. He seemed to
    believe
their language was his, to keep alive.
It was in him an exoneration. For such remarks as the one above,
when I came to understand it,
I would have carried him on my back,
out of his ruins.

I have a neighbour, along the hillside,
an old woman who loves to read.
She goes to bed early, and I imagine that when she is tired
she folds her glasses on the bedside stand
and then her arms, in the same way, on her punctured chest,
and is at rest. Now at dawn, this woman shouts
into the paddocks, and her dog shouts back. It tells her
to exult. She has her fulfilment.
What appears to be an armful of wattle is brought to us here
at daybreak and at nightfall,
lightly, without piety or desert – I see it being carried for me
from the rim of the world,
among the bushland's broken foliage.
And I had wondered, while wandering in the mazed ways of
    last night,
how I was to reach
the light again. Then I realized
that where I found myself, amid all the emphasis
on stasis,
can be seen through, as a delusion. It vanished from me, like
    eluding a theme
in the *glissando* of a violin.

Our imagination is something more dreadful than the truth,
although it is an essential affliction.
Take Deiphobus, who was called 'bashful'
in Dryden's rendering
of his story, since he was beautiful, but his nose and ears had
    been sliced off,
and he knew it was Helen,
his wife, who had betrayed him, beside her first husband
    Menelaus.
(I suppose she felt
that she had beauty enough for them both.)
Such knowledge, it was conjectured,

meant he must live
for the extent of a hundred lifetimes, to be rid of animus.
In life, everything is insecure and arbitrary,
we've innumerable opportunities
for taking affront.
The only solution is not to be.
The dead exist for none but the living. If we pursue them
their souls smell in Hades. We turn away.
They are ashes to ashes and dust on the wind.

Robert Gray

Royalty

for millad Gudanji Miller & Raggatt mob

I drove out bush with family
again to Jayipa
            a catfish hole lined
    with paperbark and river gum
and those gleaming quartzite outcrops
    like a silver and zinc plinth encompassing
                dark sheet water:

we hopped, stinging, across the baked
    earth, a tessellated black
soil with small sand drifts gathering
    to the decaying stone-boiled edges:

            and while nana fired
a billy, weaving
    pandunus frond sieves
we all crashed, energised
            in the brown water's warm wash:

    in the late afternoon
cool relief as pop arrived to dig
a bush-turkey ground-oven
    we all set to work:

            the boys
        took a cast net and hand lines
                for barra
while the girls hunted
            in water, feeling
    in the mud
for waterlily bulbs, onions and yams:

later they tap-danced the mud
    sweetening our outlook –
        a seismic detection service reading
    for hibernating turtles –
a shelled familial finery:

    at nightfall
our guts tight
with their fill we fired
        the billy and traced
    stars as pop smoked us
in quandong, picking us up:

    and nana sang country, rousing
            the scrub
and a rainbow's payback on this mine's seepage,
and another's foreshadowed hole in our burial grounds,
    mucking us up
    making us sick.

*Millad: is Kriol in the Gulf region of northern Australia for the first
person plural pronoun: we, us, our.*

*Gudanji: one of four surviving Indigenous language groups in the
Northern Territory's Gulf of Carpentaria.*

Phillip Hall

Cultural Precinct

Reflecting on Tarnanthi, a Festival of Contemporary Aboriginal and Torres Strait Islander Art.

All this creating speaking breathing on Kaurna country demands more than just an acknowledgment of a peoples past present and future, for this place, this space, is abundant with stories and strong families who have always had agency, moving through and resisting what this particular cultural-precinct represents: Tarnanthi - *rise, come-forth, spring-up, appear* – right here, in this potent-place, you will find Festival offerings beyond a feast of art, for this cultural-precinct along Adelaide's North Terrace is no easy place for everyone to navigate…. these limestone walls whisper a conglomerate fragmented journey that has lead us, toward this day, surrounded by precious gifts like these images, these hanging skirts, these glass bush-yams, these baskets, and now, in this moment, I call on you to reflect on the very walls from which they hang….

these limestone walls   frame institutions of power
shape the main story   this colonial 'free' State   /
these North Terrace statues   bronzed famous faces
symbols of colonialism   Empire-revered   /   next door
the Parade Ground   original quarry   raw materials
morph   grand buildings abound   /   limestone mined
from this old Kaurna campsite   Red-Kangaroo stories
ripped from the ground   /   *these limestone walls*   *these
limestone walls*   /   consider this Armory   that
housed a morgue   cells and gallows   watch our people
hang   /   see mounted police   perform military
functions   'pacified' our warriors   on colonial
frontiers   /   these wretched walls   this Armory
building   hear horses-hooves gallop   on cobblestoned

blood   /   this limestone heritage   revered cultural-
precinct   our bodies stolen   de-fleshed and preserved
/   *these limestone walls*   *these limestone walls*
/   consider this place   the *South Australian Museum*
their proudest collection   wins the Empire's great race
/   an uncanny replica   London's *Natural History*
Museum   but what is 'natural'   about their history of
this place?   /   they 'set up camp'   on great
expeditions   to study and collect us   'experts' in
teams   /   their cabinets of curiosity   their objects
and specimens   their racialised hierarchy   our human
remains   /   *these limestone walls*   *these limestone*
walls   /   the Migration Museum   was the old
Protector's Office   the Rations Depot   the Colonial
Store   /   blankets and flour   sugar and tea
the removal of children   the first Kaurna school   /
and behind the Art Gallery   the Radford Auditorium
the ammunitions-store   for military-police   /   then a
storage-place   for Aboriginal Records   where paper-trails
trace   surveillance and control   /   consider
the paperwork   the archiving process   to consign and
classify   this resource maintained   /   consider this
fantasy   monolith-archive   its stunning all-knowing
so easily sustained   /   *these limestone walls*   *these*
limestone walls   /   strive to navigate   this violent
place   be still and listen   there are waterholes here
/   these fresh water springs   flow a limestone-memory
erode and expose   our truth will appear.

Natalie Harkin

Tinnitus

5,000 angels dance on a pin
creating a thin, high-pitched singing
in the empty area of my ear,
plucking each high harp string
in a Morse of ping and whistle;
I can hear the whistle
but can't discern the music,
suffer its relentless din – day
into stinging night into day.
It can't be cured the doctors say
so they play audiologists' tricks
to fool my brain. My curative sound's
the shilly-shallying of surf,
of water fussing and trembling
on sandy shores, or flopping
a susurrus over rocks. You can hear froth
laced to the surfaces of sound.

For a year I've listened
to this slumbrous rustling cure,
surf splashed in the computer's core,
gushed through the car's soft speakers,
water thrushed over my head
in whispering sleep.
And still the angels sing
their dog whistle tingling,
their unchanging I-Ching,
the shrill denizens of my inner ear.
A thousand pins drop tinkling
down cliffs of ice, and zing
again in a tympani of feeling;
for folly is as folly does:
this brain is not for fooling.

Dennis Haskell

Archive Fever ~~Making Tracks~~

                    the *arkhē* appears in the nude—Jacques Derrida

You are ~~I am~~ a tracker bent ~~crouched~~ close to the page ~~ground~~
    looking
for traces and signs that sense ~~you~~ has ~~have~~ passed this way

You sniff ~~sniffing~~ for the scent of absence ~~you~~
but above all feel~~ing~~
for the gap in your ~~my~~ life
~~that wants to fill this page~~
~~alone~~

The air is incandescent

The white page ~~track~~ glows

Emptiness talks back talks back talks back
to the heat that cracks open the world ~~ground~~

This is a land of surfeit and lack
of hardness and clarity of image
of absence that opens out
or closes up the world
and sometimes the heart.

Dominique Hecq

Derrida, J 1998 Archive Fever: A Freudian Impression. Chicago: University of
Chicago Press. Trans Eric Prenowitz, p. 92.

Black Dress

For TAW

This black dress
is also a painting—
it hangs on a wall
where light holds it close.
It's a doorway to places
no-one quite knows;
that bloom and rain
with extravagant vistas.

We've sometimes entered
into the painting
dipping dark hats,
watching children
riding down lanes
(their slit-eyed scrutiny
prickling our backs),
finding a house
made out of art—
colourful images; chaotic signs—
and in a long room
have seen a black dress.

Approaching the work
we've watched ourselves there,
climbing through streetscapes,
avoiding riders
and ducking rain,
entering a house
made out of painting,
finding a room
with a black dress inside.

Now standing here,
outside of the image,
the dress seems mute
hung on its wall;
yet inside the painting,
through folds like a curtain,
we glimpse narrow laneways.
The sound of rain
is prickling our backs.

(from 'Pictures at an Exhibition')

Paul Hetherington

Relocation of the Big Prawn

Cutting you loose was always the Big Hernia,
five crustacean manholes and an ocean view semaphore.
Severing yourself at the canticles was the angle grinder's delight,
guide lines and trophy wives scrapping for a slice of spine.
Upmarket seashells splitting effigies of you,
spraying mantis spilling multiple eulogies in reverse.
Downtown, cranes shrapnel our deep dream limelight,
tethered to the countenance of primordial withers.
Hindenburging the Baudelaire was just a serving suggestion,
the dust of syphilitic kings sulphuring the contradictory.
Negativity these days means 'how to deflect light',
Gulliver's Travels ghostwritten by miniature Don DeLillos
sepia the distillation of several small children into Norfolk grog.
I want to swim upstream like a deathwish, through permafrost,
     to Canada.
Relocation means taking it offshore. So we flush out the interior
and reroute the Pacific. Seared to the pig iron of a new beginning,
we becalm posterity, pop their eyes out on stalks. In the tunnels
of a granite bedroom I wrestle and tug. Misreadings underwritten
by fantasy gambling—the stochastic improbability of this whole
thing being true. Of an evening I thrash responses to the electric
field, parry the overdetermined placenta of hair, miasma, sweat.
In the absence of fixed references, you avoid me and I prefer it.
Too much proximity fills my holes with lungs. I dissolve to be,
scuppered in the inevitable playlist, half-lunged in the backflip
of the ocean suite pedestal. At reception, the welder's pen hustles
while I swing, huddled in the roof space of countries old and lost.
Down below, henchmen fiddle with the drains, swearing like nuns.
The new guy severs a number of feelers, wonders—what fresh
apothecary will bleed this mother's tongue? An old hand floats
to the surface, joins us at last in the reappearance of our long-lost
juvenilia. The number of relationships formed on the basis

of a single misinterpretation is how the apical resorption
of the skeleton explains a decrease of the kype in kelts.
When the hacktivists come we'll scrub our hands with lemon,
warm water, blood, Greyhound ourselves senseless on a dirge
bound for Ballina, where the replacement of your breeding
teeth will make love to the hygienic cruelty of my Titles,
Feedback, Loops. In the hinterland, we'll build an art gallery
that truly *shreds*, draft a tell-all sign for the soothseer's
window in open source aspidistra sans. We'll feel nervous
about the past and nostalgic for the future, skywrite the word
jukebox in bits of broken. In the cubby of a keyhole winter we'll say
the right words are hanging from the trees, each one a fruit
of historical strangeness. In September, we will cut down
their bodies, wind their salutations into sheets.

Fiona Hile

Modern Woman Sonnets

(Labé 21; 20; 11)

What places a man beyond comparison? What shape
and shade and look drives us to despair the least
circuitously, without the patience pace
for comedy or tragedy?

What playlist most befits the whole
man, who can he outsource his outpouring to, who
still plays the lute, who could be Nature for him?

Let's say we are, at least, a breath-piece
with a sex a gait a tract and a brain upturned
and we each can know one thing at a time
and this is mine:
all the art that improves on the world
has a tinkling-nóthing effect
on lust's blue hot blue overruns.

There's a face precise from the deep's allowance:
the stranger on a sofa I knew just once,
the pristine first sight before the second sight
that love claimed with its almost-claws.

Seeing how he loved me hard
I took pity, utter, and then fell despite,
in the valley of the young and well

in a lot of little hurries, detailed rushes
in a dearth of field. Grey green *incertidumbre.*

But as I watch now the low-pressure system
massing darkness its gale-forces
smearing stars, I wonder who-what did finely
    arrange
my shipwreck on my rocks, then *en plein air*
cross-hatched from cliff-top in thin ink the scene.

\

How lovely your eyes and their looking,
small gardens with sex-minded flowers. . . .
into flesh *le fleche de l'amour* shot from
their shaded bowers. My gaze was holding, calling
wrongly your bluff, me and the blown rose
and its fresh interpetals of air.

So I've cried my days down the days-drain!

You my eyes were lit lucky objects of his eyes
but you my heart—meat!—with your surface-envy
retreated past red past desolation,
till that first replication which was desolate. . . .
Let none believe I'm a single cell at ease,
not when my heart and eyes can't share
a good or bad or neutral word.

LK Holt

The change room

This morning, walking almost naked
from the change room toward the outdoor heated pool,
I become *that man* again, unsettling

shape to be explained.
Such questions aren't asked to my face. Children
don't mean anything by it, supposedly, so I

shouldn't feel as I do,
as my bones crouch into an old shame I thought
I'd left behind. Chlorine prickling

my nostrils, a stranger
compliments me on my tattoos and shows me hers –
a dove in flight over a green peace sign –

as if the canvas was unremarkable.
She turns and limps away,
and something makes a moment of sense.

I lower myself into our element
and swim, naturally
asymmetrical and buoyant. Quite some time

later, showering, the man beside me
is keen to chat – how many laps we've each done,
how long I've lived in this town, the deep

need for movement.
Speaking, our bodies become solid.

Andy Jackson

The Jews of Hamburg Speak Out

Voyage of the Damned (SS St Louis, 1939)

To all those who seek asylum, do not think
         we have forgotten you.
Four months before the boil on Europe's knee
burst open, we were thin with hope like you,
                              sallow with stars
and reeling from Krystallnacht, whose terror
                    was untranslatable. We fled.
The ship transporting us through the dark
raised a sham swastika up its mast.
            I recall, one time, standing on the stern
under a sky that did not smell of death
as the tail of Germany diminished
            to a speck.
Such luxury on board! Cut glass and chandeliers,
but even so,
            they turned us away at Havana, you know.
The doors clanged shut, the inns all full; the same old story
at port after port. Our ship retreated with a vertebral groan,
sailing east towards the death camps of home,
            whose gates swung open to receive us.

Lisa Jacobson

Plot Points

On the rafting ice
The afterbirth of seals
Leaves stains like pink blancmange.
Glyco proteins in the fish
Keep them from freezing.

M13 in Hercules
Is a globular star cluster –
A glitterball that my mother
Could have danced the Charleston under.
She had lovely hands.

Renoir, choosing models, always looked
At their hands first.
After the war, at Lodz,
On a tour of the concentration camp,
Rubinstein said 'I was born here.'

In Melanesia, the House of Memories
Contains the treasures of the tribe.
The Somme chalk was good for tunnels.
When the barrage broke them,
The parapet bags spat white.

At Kokoda, the treetop phosphorescence
Turned the night to Christmas.
The Aussies in Tobruk
Brushed dust from bully beef.
In the dry valleys of Antarctica
Dust is raised by the katabatic wind.

With the *Wehrmacht* stalled in front of Moscow,
Even the grease froze. The 88s
Were jammed by their own shells.
Rasputitsa was the mud
Of spring thaw and autumn rain.

On a hard day in the Alhambra
The Sultan sent an apple
To the virgin of his choice.
The logo on your Macbook
Is an echo of the manner
In which Alan Turing killed himself.

In the battle for Berlin
The last panzers were overrun
Before they reached the start-line.
A dead hippo in the *Tiergarten*
Had an unexploded mortar bomb
Sticking out of its side.

While you were reading this
Millions of stars moved closer
Towards their own extinction
So many years ago –
But let's believe our eyes:
They say it's all here now.

Clive James

First contact, Kakadu

Leichhardt's grasshopper

And then one wet season there
you were. Lightning-child, improbable
creature feeding, secreted

on red rock, blue sky articulating
brick-red-ink-blue limbs, clefted
close to January waterholes

where locals plunged and carried on
as if there were nothing extraordinary
about that Sunday afternoon, as if

it weren't the first and last time
we would see you. Surrounded by a high-pitched
insect-churring in the scented aromatics

you were eating, voraciously, head tilted
above a shrug of denim shoulders. Intense
vibrato resonated. We felt as much

as saw your tensile antennae
sounding, sensing something out there
far beyond us, this improbable future.

Virginia Jealous

Diary of an Anti-elegist

1.
Even poetry dements in the end; fatal attractions to dank earth
and ash albums don't fool or buy time. Poetry cherry-picks memory
for its own ends; yet that's a medicated narcissism for some.
Earnest elegies are often rejected by dogs and children.
Listen to them howl. Voting for life outside of ritual.
I'm on your side; I'm with the hounds and the kids.
I won't let elegy make you over into a bad oil painting,
don grief's sack cloth pantomime.
Next time I see you walking down the street, checking for spot fires
in unseasonal autumn heat, light fidgeting up the shape of you
between drunken ghost gums, I will laugh and say:
the death of my father
has not made a poet out of me,
no, not yet.

2.
One thing: If you do the clanking chain and sheet,
let it be pure sight gag.
The quiet wit of the dead is yours. We expect nothing less
than theatre-restaurant ghoul. Our task, to entreat you
to turn up late to a Xmas of bad bon-bon jokes
and re-gifts. We will be waiting, in sodden crepe crowns,
drinking from someone else's warm stem glass, rare cooked animals
pressing down on First World intestines. All of us vying
to claim you. When it's too ha-ha or too sad I will bang my glass,
as ageing relatives blow fluoro party whistles,
hoping they'll be first off the sinking ship. Before she jumps,
one loved aunt flushed with booze
and sundowner syndrome, confides *en passant*:
the death of your father
has not made you a joke teller,
no, not yet.

3.
You chose a plain pine box, authenticated lightness
a clear and quick return. Death's a quick diet in that respect,
though the anorexic spookhouse cheapens –
neither sums you up nor summons you.
Most days, light and lightness refuse to pun.
Meanwhile, daylight's broken projector screens your old movie
in fits and starts, in the shady zones. I guard my ticket jealously,
fighting the light to scratch you out of faded Kodachrome.
Some days I catch sight of you sweeping leaf litter
down the coppery tow paths of late afternoon.
You always put a plant in the earth the moment it was
given to you. Weighted it in. Now I am putting you in,
not as swiftly as you would have liked.
You have no technique I hear you say. *Build it up around the bole.*
Water it in, pat it down. That way it will flourish.
I laugh and say: the death of my father
has not made a gardener of me,
no, not yet.

A. Frances Johnson

In Flight Entertainment

'no more blues', that's not a promise
there's no traction or policy in the blues

all those bars are too long a cycle
to make for twittering views

no more plaints or graces
no thanks, 'watch and listen carefully'

enhanced performance, premium economy
'a loss of consciousness', 'oxygen will flow', 'settle back'

it's a field day under the smoky hills

what does my tray table say about me
the colour of my life jacket, indeed, my life

'woke up this morning', that line's been used
an immense dark blue sea nothing like the Pacific

it's a long way down, it's a long way home
even the clouds are small

perhaps something scary or precious
will break loose as the screens fall

what if there were no more blues
everything white and cloudy, 'nothing to see here'

does Europe seem safe
there are checks again in the Schengen zone

'strong margins', more landings on Lesbos
ancient songs for peace, love, weddings, thanks

'persons of interest', abductions
the last Commodore rolls out of the factory

what do you do with your hands
time is pressing, 'enjoy the service'

'the cost of complexity', alive in the aisles
'full of self belief', 'materials handling'

showers in Cape Town, sunny and dry in Lima

your own youtube channel must be full of likes as well as gripes
as the news disappears into itself, by jings it's hard

but not so hard as no more blues

and there's New South Wales or whatever it was
or will become, cultivated white squares and a haze

'being a personal trainer', 'a true Aussie lifestyle'
from Port Macquarie to Wagga Wagga

which state would you settle in

'the Australian dream ticks all the boxes'
welcome to the Gold Coast, five minutes from the beach

no more blues, it's all white from now on
'a loss of consciousness', 'settle back' –

Jill Jones

takk for alt

they line up neatly

like a class best behaved
no whispering today

there's a view of the sea
earshot of the factory

the road lies still
the fjord is still
are two stillnesses the same?

*

not every Hardanger gravestone says
but it's the most common thing carved

thanks for everything
is the loose translation

for what is it thanks can be given?

*

tell me the sky – how it is, one more time
tell me the stream's strong words
say after me
what I have meant
you know the things to do
they're day-by-day
known to season

there is the need for a fresh coat of paint
remember to bring in the washing, the cat
(how many cats ago was that?)
and haul the boat before the storm

end of the day know all is done

du lever i vart minne
still living in our memories

høyt var du elsket
you much loved

there's thanks for being dead as well
for getting out of the way
(no one puts that on a stone)

*

stand longer in my silence here
for it is love to stand

go with the mountain in my boots
because you have a touch of sky

the colour goes out of it
sky down and earth up
everything tending to night

*

here turf is weather
and weather's a roof
my day and my night one

all are bones
clean as the dark to which we whistle
or else I'll be damned

Kit Kelen

Limbo

Why shouldn't a miracle be at the primary school disco
lurching up the dancing queue of the limbo line
where the father of Jayden, the boy with cerebral palsy,
has his arms hooked under his son's, so the boy's almost
walking, almost
dancing
when every boy and every girl, all around the limbo world
is getting ready to shimmy under that broomstick?
The DJ is a seventeen year old kid
in a rainbow vest his mum made him.
He's holding the stick.

I'm watching, for nothing other than the hope
that he doesn't raise it when Jayden's turn arrives
that he keeps it steady as the music says Hey,
how low can you go? and one by one the kids tilt
their supple spines backwards, hair dangling,
the jerk and eye-roll, the shudder of splayed muscle
as Chubby Checker croons *liiiimmmmbbbboooo*

till it's Jayden's turn; his dad drops to one heavy knee,
slips a hand behind his son's head
and shimmies him under and through - contorted, crooked -
then back up somehow
while the DJ holds that stick immoveable, no sleight of hand
and the man does not duck his own head or scramble under
so I can only think - focussed on tipping his boy carefully
into the world beyond, unscathed –
that this father, flexed hard in awkward genuflection
passed through that solid wooden hurdle
that it dissolved for a single second as his barrel chest breasted it
because, still cupping the frail tendons of his son's neck,
he was suddenly on the other side.

Cate Kennedy

Spatial Realignment of Jam Tree Gully (John Kinsella)

asphalt

asphalt   asphalt   asphalt   asphalt
ant empire 1

caltrop outbreak
rounded corner

cluster of quartz
rock dragons

RESERVE

false fence   false fence   crossover

wattlefestgate
crossover

distended boundary

arena reclamation
York gum saplings
free-ranging

gravel drive runoff
erosion

seedling sandalwood in sluices
latching on to York gum roots

paddock plantings (thriving)

ant empire 2
wattles
roos sheltering

Granites interwoven jam tree saplings ridge

ancient wind-bent
gnarled York gums

ant empire 3
RED SHED

ant empire 4

RESERVE
dead trees

granite boulder overlooking
granite boulder protecting

terrace

echidna balled and projecting
potent quills

                              roos grazing

              terrace   well 1

                                    well 2

den   90 000-litre
holes   tank (life) HOUSE
                    terrace/bank

                              lemon tree

GREAT YORK GUMS

                    GREAT YORK GUM with bees

                                        bird gully
                                        bird gully
                                        bird gully
                                           bird gully
                                        bird gully
                                        bird gully
                                        bird gully
                                        bird gully
                                        bird gully
                                        bird gully
                                        bird gully
                                        bird gully

dead territory
drought residues
greyed trunks

              bent trees/run-off damage/
              slalom from gradient
              filled with rocks
              to slow erosion   ant empire 5

dense tangle of confused trunks (living and dead), termite-ridden
                      stubble quail sheltering   **STEEP BANK**

                      NEIGHBOUR

fence fence fence fence fence fence fence fence clutter of detritus fence

      RESERVE

John Kinsella

Getting away with it

It started as a joke.
I couldn't write anything, so I
stole a few short lines

from Robert Creeley,
then drove real fast
without considering the desti-

  nation.
Soon Basho's frog was leaping
out of a woodblock

& into my notebook, though
I wasn't crazy enough to toss
Elizabeth's fish back into the sea.

Before I could cite the cento defense,
I'd won the Blake, the Newcastle
& the Ethel Malley urn. Now

the truth is out, I'm crawling
through the stink
of a sewer, struggling

  to breathe.
The bottom rungs of the ladder
are impossibly high,

while a sniper waits
near the manhole to blow
my head off.

I dress in my shame every day—
a suit of beautiful words
I long to call my own.

Andy Kissane

Foxstruck

Dinner done, dishes draining, the fire
a red glow in its dark box, I step outside
beyond the porch light, the grass
stiff with frost in the home paddock,
the night sky shelved but for the bright paw
and nose of the Dog Star chasing a hare
in the scudding dark, the almost
forgotten name of a flagship tossing
into view in a time before typhoid,
cholera and sweetened damper, the gorge
rising in the dip where shots rang out
last night, our feral neighbour licensed to
kill anything that moves, floodlit
and whooping just beyond our fence line,
which a deer can clear in a moment if only
she knew she'd be safe here, but what's a fence
in a forest of stars? The cold eats fingertips
and ankles. If I had flares, I would light them.
Makes no sense how we got here. Makes
perfect sense: a fox, frozen, almost
touching me. Three red paws on the ground,
one white lifted in mid-step, a thousand
tiny hairs aspark in the moonlight.
Breath a small vapour, electric.
Eyes like river stones, that old language
of fire held high in the brush-stroked tail
pulsing between us, two feet of charged
ground sunk without sound in a heartbeat,
the mist made mystic at knee-height.
Foxstruck. Standing alone in a paddock
pouring electricity under a night sky
blinking cold atoms without answer,
blood quickening the slow burn of fox,
tricky as history, the fire before and after.

Shari Kocher

Bringing It All Back Home

*After Allen Ginsberg's First Party at Ken Kesey's
   with Hell's Angels*

Hot black night thru melaleucas –
cars rest in moons of yellow
fallen from poles that hiss and burr –
and stars blaze above in navy linen.
The tops of flame trees breathe
insects that drift in the warm breeze.
And parents in the drive, tend

barbecue and smoke (acacia, gum),
pretending happiness, but their eyes belie.
Their tired son in leather jacket sweats
the cool and itches in the dark, rubbing
tobacco and weed, furtive in corners
while other leather jacketed boys smoke
dope under the front yard citreodora –

purposeful, concentrated – and way
too cool for school. I cross the lawn
and beer can litter to climb the porch steps.
Two boys in army shirts slump
at the screen door, half-hearted guards,
smoked-out, listless and benign
like domestic cats.

Their girls dance. One in scarlet tights
and long dress, sweat in her hair,
kisses an energetic boy, who leans
in to her on the lounge floor.
Her boyfriend guard doesn't notice,
he looks across the lawn, stoned,
smiling a welcome like Buddha.

Others talk on couches, but most
move to the music – twenty of them –
to the vibration thru the floor.
They sway in the middle of the room
and bend like Vietnamese huts in wind.
I join them and lift my arms
to the new, sudden rush of sound

like war, the beat we came for.
Pounding, shrill, the music charges,
electric, we rock and shift like choppers
in a storm. A red-haired boy,
tight-jeaned, moves like Nureyev.
He smokes a roach, eyes shut.
I look at his crotch and want to marry.

Simeon Kronenberg

Kangarilla, Summer, 2016

There's the creek, the white road, and the woodlot,
where trees long planted stretch now for clean sun;
and – light's conjurement – there's the summer's throw
of half-gold grass upon the stilled breast of
the hill: but hunkered under that, eruptions
in the mantle, rocks that are the real deal,
the bone inside the meat. We meet each morning
for the hard work of the day: pick, spade, wrench,
wire, drills like noisy arrows straight into the wood,
to prick the land with relics of our time.
We're of an age now where the comfort's in
neat excellence when the task's complete.
Chaos once cast charm. It doesn't now.
We lift and dig and grip as balm to loss of joy.
And everywhere and nowhere is the boy.

Verity Laughton

Wax Cathedral

Two shot glasses, lit from within
by sixteen year old Lagavulin.
A lemon tree, cut back with the imprecision
only a bread knife can bring
to organic joinery.
A magpie lark that lost its one-
winged mate, and who then
imprinted on her memory
despite being shunned, melodically.
These things occupy the end of each day
now that we are settled
in the house we call Wax Cathedral
named for the way
light makes the walls run and pool
to where shadows should be gathering
like evidence of the time we spend
on departures and arrivals
that play themselves out, daily.
Yet light prevails, in corners
and on skirting boards
like thin applications of saffron paint
and where a tree has survived
our ministrations, a bird avoids a life
of hearing itself, which always leads
to mimicry. And before the rooms
have darkened, atramentously
we turn our lamps on
the weave in their linen shades
like screen-printed rain
our glasses shot through with afternoon light.

Anthony Lawrence

Blow Job (kama sutra)

Made in Heaven series, Jeff Koons 1991

She and he are the yellow of daffodils,
canaries, Smiley faces, margarine or
Post-it® notes, Sponge Bob, tennis balls,
piss in snow or a warm golden shower.

He stands before her in act of faith,
his shaft caressed by the lemon Venus:
she takes his person into her mouth
in an act of throat-loving oral congress.

Blown in glass it is eternal primavera
in this paean to the pleasures of the tongue:
deep flexion and a repertoire of licks, a
shameless urge to suckle like the young –

a hunger comes upon me. O lord, please
feed me – I'm going down on my knees.

Bronwyn Lea

Poem

Adultery fucks a family up as much as poverty
Because the memories can't run away from home
That's a lot of hatred from a mother
Nothing I'd care to discuss right now

Because the memories can't run away from home
Once a kid learns guilt he's going to stumble
Nothing I'd care to discuss right now
Never grew any taller, just sadder and angrier

Once a kid learns guilt he's going to stumble
I quit school to escape the staring eyes
Never grew any taller, just sadder and angrier
I know that nobody ever changed history, but I had to try

I quit school to escape the staring eyes
The sun, the silence, the nothingness
I know that nobody ever changed history, but I had to try
Part of what makes me interesting for science

The sun, the silence, the nothingness
It was like an acid eating into me
Part of what makes me interesting for science
You're beautiful. What's the emergency?

It was like an acid eating into me
No sexual act ever commenced, instead I trashed the room
You're beautiful. What's the emergency?
Everyone's got their own version of the truth

No sexual act ever commenced, instead I trashed the room
Just want to see if property feels pain
Everyone's got their own version of the truth
Maybe some day, but not today

Just want to see if property feels pain
It's going to end in infinity, and if there is no infinity
Maybe some day, but not today
Can't stop love from doing its damage

It's going to end in infinity, and if there is no infinity
That's a lot of hatred from a mother
Can't stop love from doing its damage
Adultery fucks a family up as much as poverty

Emma Lew

Lovestore

To request the presence or attendance of
to wish for, long (*to be, have, do*)
'toe a line' meaning stand in a row

Of things requisite
a vehement pang
       eyther of bodie or mynde
pursuit of paltrie trash
a fit, outburst or state of strong excitement

Amorous impulse, lewd behaviour (*obs.*)
senses relating to passivity and activity
affections, tropes and intimate apparel
limping made (un)conditional

Thy darling sin which to enjoy thou couldst
resist all others (least thou thinkest so)
frigidity, the proper passion of water,
       sometime accidentally hot

Kate Lilley

A House in Switzerland

Dignitas, Zurich

So this is what it comes to: a small blue corrugated house
set in sifting snow. After months of planning, self-argument,

all agonies exchanged for innocuous things:
two wineless glasses, a space to sign your name.

The last decision is kindly trivial (milk, dark or praline?) –
a closing sweetness for the mouth. You know how it should go:

the first draught to dull the stomach for that second blow.
But even the nub of melting on your tongue can't mask

what's just been swallowed. Your insides buck, surprising you.
A late request for water is denied; it would undo everything.

And so it ends with this: your dying wish a sip of water
and all around the falling snow.

Debbie Lim

Possibly

How's Possibly doing today?
She's okay, she's possibly
recovering from a possible asthma attack.
What's Possibly doing? The impossible,
That's what. Attending to twenty students
some of whom will possibly fail
tasks Possibly set which they feel
are impossibly high.
Possibly is cooking dinner for ten
and being polite in impossibly demanding
situations. Possibly would like to take a break
from her situation but can't possibly
because she needs the money.

Her impossible husband
will possibly rock up for Christmas
needing money and certain other things.
Possibly talks to me
about Milton and Sophocles.
She brings in the washing laughing
knowing she'll possibly manage
and between the cracks of impossible demands
find happiness sometimes sitting
at our picnics drawing the headland
which resembles an ancient Roman.

Kate Llewellyn

Pastoral /

'Asset management'

                    winter once more   and still
        the grapevine's crimson
              leaves veil
      the front fence
       as the number-cruncher
    declares
  'you should cut that back—
    it's a classic
  white picket
you've got there'

Cameron Lowe

Orchards

(Melissa Parkes' parents had an apple farm in W.A.,
Julie Bishop's a cherry farm in S.A.)

When she met the Christians Bishop had arrested
for protesting detention of refugees, Parke
wore a coat like apple blossom: pink,
white and green, translucently. Bishop
on the day the Bali two were transferred
to the death island wore a dress
the colour of cherry blossom, dark pink,
looked gaunt with anxiety. Politics
will pierce you with its empathy, if you
practise it successfully. Apple flowers
spread raggedly and openly, breeze
dapples through them. Cherry blossom
reblooms so densely, brilliantly, that we
plant temples to ensure its resurrection.

Jennifer Maiden

Intimacy

During the French film,
I spend my time wondering
how I can put doors and windows into poems.

The director shoots them
always straight on, so they frame
the old man and woman in the film like pictures.

Really I'm trying not to think about ageing.
The woman in the film gets dementia,
spends her time on an electric bed.

Fewer people will ever see this film
then saw Briana Loves Jenna,
which is the tenth-bestselling adult DVD of all time.

In it, Briana loves Jenna
orally, mammarily, vaginally and anally
for close to an hour.

No one enters or exits the room.
Or maybe they do
and I had left the room where we were showing it.

By that point, it's hard to keep straight
the g-string, porn and cigar parties
we threw for our fifteen-year-old feminism;

hours spent deep-throating brush-handles,
looking for our epiglottises in mirrors
that fogged up like windows.

The old man in the French movie
is changing his wife's diaper,
directly over his shoulder is a window,

you can't tell if she can see out of it.
In her autobiography Jenna Jameson
uses the word 'wee-wee' instead of penis,

like "he had a big 'wee-wee'" or "he took out his 'wee-wee'",
her vagina is a 'pussy', never a window,
but it often opens doors, so she says.

The man comes back from behind the door,
we see his face for a second.
I hadn't realised how I'd missed him.

I forget so many things,
we were so young, I remember.
And so tender.

Caitlin Maling

Visitation on Myrtle Street

I was woken at some hour
of darkness before dawn by a scent so heavy
on my senses, on the room, that I was convinced

a burglar had broken in
and was loitering
upstairs or in the hallway, or having caught

my step on the stairs above him was lying low
in the laundry, or sitting
upright and unbreathing

in one of the Windsor chairs, unaware it was
his scent that betrayed him.
I checked the door to the balcony, then the door

to the street with its double lock. In the dark front
    room I checked
the sofa. Stretched full length
on its French blue he'd be hard

to detect. No one was there
but the scent was overpowering. 'What kind
of scent?', K would enquire

at breakfast. 'Was it
musk? Was it pine?' 'No, something sweeter – why
do you ask? Something sharper, maybe cheaper.'

'Because that would tell us,' he told me
seriously, 'what kind
of angel you were visited by.' 'Here?'

I protest. 'In Myrtle Street?' 'Why
not?' I took it in. Sometimes I wake to the smell of coffee
being brewed downstairs. It wakes me. Why not

the smell of an intruder?
When I woke again the scent had faded. What
had not was the change I felt

on my skin, on my nerves.
Later I worked for an hour or two
at my desk, struggling with angels

of another sort, who leave
no trace I would call a scent. Of musk or sweat,
or pine. Only pen-strokes on a page

they have changed with their lingering, when they deign
to linger. Or a dazzling
blankness when they do not.

David Malouf

Invisible Cities

i)
Back home from hospital again.
You read *Invisible Cities* outside
in the morning sun. A small lizard appears.
Its solar-powered musculature moves
across the paving stones. Its skin is both matte
and jewelled in the sunlight. It stops and flicks
its front legs down to its sides, like an ingenious
Edwardian gadget snapping itself shut.
You and the creature take in the sun, then
the lizard heads for the maze of grass,
hiding from the hard-nosed suburban birds.
You take yourself indoors into the dark of the house,
clutching Calvino, the old fabulist.

ii)
Later, the sun performs its drawn-out
power-down, summer already merciless.
You take the dog for a walk, its gait ginger,
while it fusses over what to piss on.
Around the corner, the audacious stadium lights
vie against the sunset. The smell of frying meat
is in the air; the bitter taste of Anginine
under your tongue.

iii)
You read at night, while a lawless wind
upsets the house. You lose your thread.
Calvino engenders fantasies. Dark staircases
frequented by music students and government men;
a forest in which night squats;
an empty Ferris wheel, with all its moral weight.

The dog in his fur
sleeps on dusty floorboards,
and twitches like a muscle.

David McCooey

Study of a Lion

In black chalk the beast
brusques forward   Silence   Rubens
has stopped his mouth
with a single line   He is already
awed by the den
he will find himself in even now
as his mane curls into wisp
of emptiness   A study on paper

But there in white chalk the grim
pose brightens
into recognition smudged nose
bent toward the scent
of viewer   Eyes steadily lighting
toward the years one swift textured paw
lifted ever so slightly
Patient as an avalanche

Kate Middleton

Craft

The craft of my enemy is my only aim
its perfect end. The great anvil is an eye, cornea hard,
good as new. The nodding tongue
agrees my discipline is fine, if tone deaf.

Not dependent on confinement
the psyche is diminished, buried, then quarried so.
One stone rests in the ear, rolls like a torso
in the new, smashed on consignment.

How can we take it, so knee deep in tragedy?
There's a circle of girls, a circle of laurels
on each blank head, perfectly voiceless. With intricate phrasing
their white clothes oscillate and vacillate, walk on by.

Bright flowers are a bride, held dearly in the breath.
Ship lights fade away, hard as sarcophagi.

Peter Minter

Nuclear Family Bees

Little native-bee hives
clotted all up the trunk
of a big tree by the river.

Not pumped from a common womb
this world of honey-flies
is a vertical black suburb

of glued-on prism cells.
Hunters stopping by
would toe-walk up,

scab off single wax houses
and suck them out, as each
smallholder couple hovered

remonstrating in the air
with their life to rebuild,
new eggs, new sugarbag,

gold skinfulls of water.

Les Murray

Shakespeare & the State Library

An avalanche, in Alaska (in
1958) caused, a tidal wave 1,740 ft high.
Diane Arbus's work (in her photographs) violated
all notions of "privacy". -- Kennel-up -- stop talking!
Bluish-black lobsters, are made red by boiling...
It slowly dawned on me, that i was the one
who was expected to somehow pull, yank, drag, get, and draw
the family out of poverty, by somehow becoming
a Doctor, or Lawyer, or something else, and that the family
would "willingly" sacrifice everything it had "for, Me"
(including, the girls); i was somehow the Great White Hope.
My My my... / Shakespeare used "my" 12,964 times (in
his plays) as in the line, My life hath some interest in this line.
It freaked me out. I didn't know, how
i was going to do it, but i knew getting an education
was part of it. A phobia, is a neurotic disorder.
I told the parents, i couldn't study here i.e. at the back of
the shop -- i had to go to the State Library (in the City), and
they agreed. (But not to make a famine, where
an abundance lies, it had to be, when the shop wasn't busy).
-- The pressure was on. -- No excuse! (Hope is the feeling
that something good, is imminent). But, what??
One day, walking up the marble-steps i saw Barry Jones (from
Pick-a-Box). It made my day; desiring this mans art, and
that mans skope. He was smart, and had brains, and
i was somehow like him, cos i was in the same building.
(But) how can i then be elder than thou art? One day,
my father (a little drunk), called me over, grabbed me by
the stomac, looked at me, and said, "When, i die --
you get Nothing!" [He lied, he cost me a funeral, and
a gambling debt, about 30 years later]. With my pocket-
money, i bought a copy of Shakespeare's Sonnets

from Collins Bookshop. O change thy thought,
that I may change my minde -- i was rapt! -- i was
in love with Greatness, and i knew this was Greatness.
O how I faint when i of you do write. It seemed
exactly how a poet, should say it. I started swimming in it,
guessing what words meant, or re-wording them (for
my own pleasure) as in, seek that beautious roofe
to... "urination", instead of that beautious
roofe to "ruinate". (Let it mangled be, for joy
delights in joy)! O that you were your selfe, -- and that last
line (in particular) struck me. In between all this,
i was studying hard, and getting smart, but Not from
the stars do i my judgement plucke, And yet me thinkes
i have Astronomy. But aside from all that
philosophy, the Sonnets were ultimately all about Love, and
they dug deep trenches in thy beauties field.
Over dinner one day, my father asked me, what i was reading.
I didn't know what to say. How could i say, To thee
i send this ambassage, in Greek? Or mine this, mine thus,
mine thee, mine must, or why should i hast
my hence (or some such)? My father, wasn't anything like
Shakespeare's, who as a decrepit father takes delight
to see his active childe do deeds of youth.
So i said, i'm reading this book by this guy
called Shakespeare. (He didn't care or know, who
Shakespeare was, and i knew it). (He was only interested, in
where the next quid was coming from, on
the gambling table). So i said, its about a bloke
who's in love with this woman, and its taken him
about 20 pages (so far), just to kiss her hand.
My father, looked up at me, and said "O"
we're up to, that stage
        are we?

π.0.

Letter from the swimming pool

we are trying to substitute
   our thoughts for these blossoms
      an always-already erotic run of
         small buds not made in our image

bouquets of plastic spoons
travel overland
to be opened in detention,
odourless murmurs
         service brought to life

threats arrive ziplocked
ridiculous like Oldenberg's
         inflatable lunch

a golf ball sinks
   amongst the harbour crud
launched from a 'private party'
   I begin collecting pins

it was the dream about

         'clients'

  in *basso rilievo*
repeated pattern becoming unreadable
   overloaded
a lobster crawls out of the waratah
   too much to be resolved in lino-cuts

wet branches make cybernetic filigrees
   or one unbroken line of paint

a map to the yams to
            purple commas up & down the brachial bone

skinned over but
            barely functioning circuitry

    tender-stemmed / granulating city
            thatch of light industry

    you can pan for gold
    in a *real* colony
    while noting civic displays of tidiness

    mushrooms grow
                            in upset ground
    slow-turning deciduousness
            crystal form data-mining in the apricot light

Ella O'Keefe

Cyborg me

first thing I'd hack would be my womb
hack it right out like the tin woodman with his enchanted axe
       put a music box in there, have it play *Greensleeves*

with my artificial lungs, I will unquit and smoke
four packets a day
print new bones as needed
       my fibre optic hair will flash like synchronised fireflies

my forehead's going to be an LED scrolling message
       sometimes it will say FUCK OFF, unprovoked
other times it will say USE YOUR INITIATIVE

robotic blood cells will allow me to hold my breath underwater
for hours, my tetrachromatic vision means I can see every colour
not invented yet, my cuttlefish skin means I can be more invisible
than usual, I will have a periscope

that comes out of my skull
       I will jump over trees like a vampire in *Twilight*
stick to windows with my gecko toepads
I will never be too cold or sad

I will write poems eight times faster, be able to smell a grizzly
in Montana, Wyoming, those kind of places
my auton fingers will be gun barrels and when I see those kids
littering or drawing penises on my fence with permanent markers
I will shoot them dead

Meredi Ortega

Ekphrasis

One thinks of how the details must converge,
the storytellers' small manipulations
across the wild millennia of firelight,

the father and the son, their unfamiliar
waxy wings, their awkward altitudes,
the sea and metal sun withholding judgement,

the young man flying (as he must) too high,
the older man more cautious over whitecaps
as artists, in their turn, who feel both callings,

the sun which lifts a youth beyond himself,
the waves below mere space between two points
which must, they know, lead on towards that more

pragmatic view designed to bring us Brueghel's
Landscape with the Fall of Icarus,
that seascape with its ploughboy on the left

who pays it no attention; and, later on,
the Auden poem, published 1940,
when young men yet again, with aluminium

wings, were plunging bravely through the air
and Breughel's 'expensive, delicate ship' had even
then and even now 'somewhere to get to'

where Daedalus and Icarus, aloft
on insubstantial wings and powering through
the tricky air, are not beyond re-use.

Geoff Page

from Hawes — God's Intruder

CP-G:
4.
Living on the Mullewa fringes
Became my people's place
When a colonial township emerged
Like a pimple amongst the wildflowers

Foreign church structures rose
Dominating the landscape
Family showed me the quarry
From which rocks were taken
Building the Whiteman's worship place
Close to the Mullewa Reserve
Mullewa—Morawa Road nearby
Aboriginal hands helped build that temple
Their energy and sweat is in them rocks
Their heart is in them rocks
Hawes didn't do it on his own
Wonder if that is written anywhere?
As a child I peered into that temple
Curious why gargoyles watched the entry
Frightened to look at the statues inside

Our playgrounds included train tracks,
Wheat silos, the Common and looking into the dam
Our family had died in there—as local kids we would
Peer through the big wire fence at the dam
Wildflower season meant tourist buses
We chased the bus from Our Lady of Mount Carmel
To the Lesser Hall for the promise
Of left-over sandwiches and cakes.

JK:
5.
On the steps of the Big Church
I hesitate, unsure of what's inside
for me. I have the sand and wheat
ships in my head, and wonder
how far they might stretch the scene.

Mum is a teacher at the high school,
and my nickname there is Dictionary.
I write poems in a laboratory.
I work weekends and holidays
in the shadows of the mineral sands
factories, preparing samples
that show the quality of the land
pouring through the capitalist
hourglass, shifting the spirit
to metals and plastics and paint.

It was rocket science. The birds
stayed away, their songs
ignored by too many. Shifting
sands. Gunslits in "settler" buildings.

We ride our bikes from Town
to Drummond's Cove where crayfish
bristle below reefs and reef sharks
patrol the gaps, snapper glinting,
brightening the underworld.

We live opposite the prison
in a limestone house
that was home to nurses,
an old colonial mansion
taken over by the Education

Department, a statement of possession
we know is haunted, distressed.
We weather a cyclone,
we find old coins fallen
through the wooden boards.
We are part of something
we can't quite piece together.
Mum volunteers to teach prisoners
written English, to listen to their lives.

Now, where house and yard
and Moreton Bay fig stood,
is Coles Shopping Centre
carpark. Beneficence?
For the people?

Down from there, trains
rounded on themselves,
head-to-tail on the turntable,
and the sea against the seawall,
and the curve of beach
reaching to Saint George's
(what did he have to do with it?)
and the cobbler's sting that undid
my nerves and had me shrieking
the agony of Champion Bay
I didn't understand. The school
was busy re-enacting Grey's
expedition but I knew
that wasn't part of my vision,
though later I'd rewrite it
as a poem of decolonisation.

When I return to Geraldton,
to what part of me is there,

I rest in a dry creek bed
and listen to the river redgums,
I go to the bottomless pool
and watch the swallows
defy gravity. I know sunsets
make a coast and I listen
hoping my errors
will find redress.

CP-G:
6.
Growing up I lived opposite the Catholic Church
"Our Lady of Mt Carmel" in Mullewa
Every day I walked past Monsignor's house
I knew nothing of their beliefs and customs
It was just a playground to take pictures
Get a cool drink from the water fountain
The gargoyles perched at the entrance did
Frightened me at night as I close my eyes
And sprinted past the church to get home—
I didn't understand why these monsters
Were on a church building—roof at that
I still don't care they just looked out of place

During the celebrated wildflower season
We would pose—"cute little Aboriginal kids"
For the tourist as we waited for rewards
Of cakes and sandwiches leftovers from
Their morning and afternoon teas
They probably felt sad for us—who knows!
We just got our feed and waved to them

I wrote poems and stories in a little diary
You know the ones with lock and key
And cute little girly covers

Each time finding new hiding places
From intruding little relatives and the rest
Each time having to tear up and throw away
My words, thoughts, emotions, feelings
Because there was no hiding places

The big church in Geraldton on the sand hill
Was not part of my world in Mullewa
It was there but meant nothing to me
I don't remember it as a child or a teenager
Why should I had no business with it?
Our SDA church sat staunchly
On Maitland Road waiting for its family
We got bags weetbix, oranges, and apples
Saved us from really starving so
That's something I guess

But that big church in Geraldton
What a poser standing there like a temple
My mum went to a wedding there in 1940s
An Aboriginal wedding at that—Catholics
I have a pic of mum leaning on outside wall
All young beautiful and a tea maid
Mum had a permit to work in Geraldton
At West End of Marine Terrace
From the Native Protection Board
Or should I say her Employer had the permit
That's the way it was—Aboriginal people
Were controlled and couldn't move freely

Even as a teenager coming across to the
Aboriginal Basketball carnivals
Or at the Maitland Park footy oval
I don't recall the Big Church
It didn't make a lasting impression

It just didn't belong to my world
Later in life I moved to Geraldton
And the big Church was in my face
I drove past it, I walked past it
I stared at it from the QPT lawns
I couldn't escape its physical presence

And what I did learn about it made me sick
The space it so grandly took over
Was once a traditional campsite
Is it coincidence that the Aboriginal
People living at the campsite were

Moved to other locations including
Moore River Native Mission?
At the same time the big takeover
Colonising church was to be built.

Oh yes the big church is grand
They pray and worship their god
Tourists come from everywhere
With their cameras to make memories

All I can think about when I see it
Is of the campsite taken over
Of our people displaced and alienated
From traditional country
Colonised space it became and stayed.

Charmaine Papertalk-Green and John Kinsella

'A Decidedly Pathological Process:

akin to falling on a pitch-
fork',[1] muscle-cut
                cutpurse
                        purse-strings
                                strings attached
                                        attachment may be
affected by birth trauma, the 'cascade
        of intervention':[2]
(*intervenire*, fr. Latin: 'to come between'
such as your small body intervened between
me and sleep or the secret pulse of fontanel
dividing skullplates)
Once you've had one episiotomy, you'll
probably need another:
(the opiate theory of surgical cuts)
(the gateway drug for the *primigravida*)
                                gravidy, parity
('our stitching and unstitching has been
naught')[3] Sutures, rows
needles like oars, close parted waters
One of these was not overheard
in the post-natal ward:
a. 'When I gave birth I had an epidural'
b. 'When I gave birth I had an orgasm'
c. 'When I gave birth I was in stitches'
    Not a stitch on, in a bright-lit room
        a stitch in time
    cross stitch ('Wanted: a needle swift
enough to sew this poem into a blanket')
        'FORK!'
I said, as well as
'It's not as bad as it sounds'

And it was not, it was not
when I was cut and sutured
    ('You can cut
                    all the flowers
but you cannot keep spring from coming').[5]

Felicity Plunkett

1 Joseph DeLee, early 20th century obstetrician, champion of the episiotomy,
   on the subject of birth
2 Sheila Kitzinger, 'the high priestess of natural childbirth'
3 W.B. Yeats
4 Charles Simic
5 Pablo Neruda

Weeping Foxes

You told, or rather warned me, that the foxes would start mating soon, and that their barks and cries would be so loud and so like a woman being strangled that I would be woken by them, but that I shouldn't worry for it would only be foxes mating in the garden.

I think it's true that there is a time belonging to listening and a time belonging to hearing and these, I believe, are different times. Perhaps they're not dissimilar to the crossing of the night and day that Heraclitus described: two strangers passing each other on intersecting paths, their heads pointed in opposite directions. There is difference in the crossing and the parting, but also similitude in the approach and the leaving. Do they, night and day, nod upon meeting? Are words exchanged? It would depend on the era, that is, depend on if time were present, or telling.

It's possible that birth could be likened to the sound of a woman being strangled, but it was no matter, no matter at all. Night passed into day—he went from me into the room—and I wondered whether the moment belonging to that precise and primordial movement was why women since Antiquity have been described as the harbingers of borders, secrets, nests and masquerades—

All those who represent birth and receive life back unto themselves somehow become unlovable as soon as they are weeping, even though mating foxes too cry out and become unsettled at what they don't recognise.

Claire Potter

Shabnam Nightwish

"You can bury them deep under, sir; you can bind them in tunnels, ...
but in the end where a river has been, a river will always be."
"Thrones, Dominations", Sayers & Walsh

                             was not the Pashtun *lur*
with sea green eyes on the cover of
National Geographic, walking back into Tora Bora,
caves of illiteracy, tunnels of childbirth,
certainty in a plum coloured burqa.

she was not the Iranian *khahar* leaning on a
street-side maple tree, marked from a rooftop
to leave herself in little red trickles on a
shaky hand-held film strewn to millions.

not the Somali *gabar* in a Dadaab tent with
litter for toys, mouthing a canister nozzle as
a teething ring, innocent to how hopes are sung
in tongues to a pin-prick moonrise.

Shabnam Nightwish, the *jinn*,
truant, cryptic and near in all these

women like subterranean rivers, latent and
drip-soaking the roots of sires and tectonic
plates, sunless seas of mothers and wives ferried
in caverns under sail of kismet or false ballot,

lagoons of womankind inverted and
weeping up to nourish others, invisible

'til visited by *Shabnam*, night-sung to merge
in culverts, protected to learn and stream

up sinkholes of knowing, reclaim their wombs
and settle on work like *shabnam*, cut furrows in
slanted fields of lore, sluice tradition from
baked clods to amaryllis flowers, take possession

and reach daylight, a liberty of sea green
whirling like smokeless fire.

Hessom Razavi

Translations:
Shabnam: 'morning dew'; Persian girls name
lur: girl (Pashtun)
khahar: sister (Farsi)
gabar: baby girl (Somali)
jinn: in Islamic Mythology, a class of spirits made from smokeless fire,
capable of appearing in various forms to possess humans in benevolent,
malign or neutral ways.

The Subject of Feeling

Outside the church, unmemoried,
names of the dearest
deserting me, I turn as they
load you in the hearse, set off
with a small police escort.

For a quarter of a century
we have been ramming you
in cars of various sorts,
long before the age
of ramps and hoists.

They took longer to prise you
from the giddified wreck –
two hours was the report.
Eschatology is a slow
remorseless science.

While they forged above
a woman squeezed inside
and stayed with you,
marvelled at your composure,
heard about a new daughter.

Then the subject of feeling –
why you had none in your feet.
Men ground the car with steel
and flung it open
like a sack of wheat.

Peter Rose

Night Watch

Time is elastic, its zenith fit to breaking
when you wait for the ambulance – now leaning over him,
now rushing back and forth from house to street straining
for sirens, night so dark and wet and quiet out there.

Listening for breath in a slight boy of fifteen years
is an ancient art requiring silence. Kneeling on your hall floor,
ear right to his lips, beside the frenzied shouts of his father,
whose panic of pacing is the only thing he can offer him.

Your own son watches his friend from the corner,
slumped, slightly beaten, the first fire of alcohol seeming
less necessary than it might have been, not worth the effort now,
while the friend he tried to carry home lies on his side, still.

Slapping his rump to try and wake him feels like assault.
Strange to be able to do things he would never allow,
ice you run across his cheeks a cruelty. Beyond limp,
he will not jerk away, open his mud-brown eyes.

When they finally come, wearied knights of the new wars,
they cannot rouse him, tell us it's not good, open his lids to
     pupils
so huge, so pitch and utterly void, his mother gasps, sinking,
and you never saw anyone so unconscious who wasn't dead.

You make your son sit and watch. They strap on an oxygen mask,
fail to open his mouth for a tongue block, quietly ask what he
     took –
vodka yes, but weed? pills? needles? No. Just vodka. Straight.
'He was kicked,' your boy says, 'they punched me in the head.'
     And vomits.

Clipped on a stretcher, they lift him out of the hall. In the long
    night,
fourteen hours twisted in tubes before he rouses, you
    remember
they loved pizza by the swimming pool for the last three
    birthdays, watched
videos, Xbox, played Star Wars with Darth Vader the only
    enemy –

and when you turned sixteen no-one had parties at all.

Robyn Rowland

Astronomical Twilight

In a dress, in a dream
your guide points out carvings, a well to kick.
Sissy mountains slope to ground.
His fans bay in the church of Perpetual Succour.
Plane to the apron,
a rook abed, to swindle and jack.

Walk into sky when the street ends, to turbid night.
Traffic dinks around a tower.
She rotates in her garden.
The spying dog returns, flummoxed.

What a relief, her promenade or whatnot
but still the shouting,
and languor overtakes both like a victim,
his velvety daub in the ashtray,
the sewn mouths in the islands.
Parliament resumes, on a corpse.
Each path, addled and peremptory, calls
in bossed waves.

Gig Ryan

Smartraveller

Just knowing those colours makes it safer
already and how they'll change anyway by the time
you, thirteen now, are old enough for elsewhere:

RED ORANGE YELLOW GREEN but not about weather
except for extremity and those are most finite
and fickle, cyclones though murderous rarely durable

as human cruelty. *Where are you going?*
the site prompts but you choose *Browse countries*
then *List all countries*, then run the current date –

not to miss anything – every day you check them
like a thing growing in the mind's garden
that needs tending, a world of worrying

for others under some degree of mastery; keep track
of flare-up, pandemic, earthquake, and ask me
sidelong, to define *civil unrest, safety and security*

though these are terms you know, as if rehearsing,
as if there could be something more the words don't
indicate, a further shade in my palette till now

held back, but I can only disappoint, being arms'-length,
and listen my best as you list the ten tallest mountains
while we head for the school bus because last night

and all this week it was Nepal, and pulling your quilt
around you to ready for sleep was rugging up
for Everest, and before that, another land, one day.

Tracy Ryan

ghosting the ghetto

for Steven

In their third floor brick flat, the one tucked into the asphalt
folds of Warwick Farm, past *El Toro* motel, down where
the winding road straightens out opposite takeaway tucker,
my grandparents were rebuilding Lebanon, and no one seemed
to mind. Every Sunday we made like pilgrims in Holden
Commodores, traversing highway homeland

to bicker and eat. As adults renewed rivalries, we kids splashed in
the Abraham River, once known as Adonis, an ancient baptismal
turquoise that cleaved through the hallway. Sometimes the country
changed with us & we climbed Mount Lebanon in the lounge,
cooling our bodies beneath old olive trees.

The tapestries were gaudy, the TV a small cube in the corner,
and smoke was forever on the air. In that, metaphor & country are
one. As with every hajj, there were too many bodies and the door
was kept open for us to spill from, an ecstasy of difference.
In this, metaphor & Arab are one: no lone place can hold
in its small clay hands so many rivers

and no Ark can contain us, whatever scripture commands.

In adolescence, the *Kaaba* flowered between us, a black square
lotus edged in gilt across the sides, doors of gold gleaming in
afternoon light. It made ants of us and the mountains and rivers,
the motels and convenience stores. Now we spoke by rote,
prayers half-memorised in the sacred hours of the insomniac,
sinking budding secrets

and the kinds of questions that can unmake family.

When the girls started to stand apart, trying to hijab
their modesty, we saw jamar t all around us, & lined our hands
with bits of rock to hurl at the devil. Only the walls were a mirage
and it was our cheeks which split beneath thrown stones. Later,
it made perfect sense to learn that in 1627, a gutter was added
to the Kaaba

to protect it from flooding. Or perhaps to stop it from blooming.

Before my grandparents began to recreate Lebanon out of ruined
cartilage, someone should have checked if they were students
of history, or if they knew their way around a map. Beirut became
Bondi became Liverpool, & the local creek behind the cricket
pitch drowned the old rivers, and new names blessed our flesh,
like Nike, Adidas, and Reebok.

Someone should have checked if they knew a flower could replace
the house of god.

Boys have no business with god, except where he can be found
in the slap of hard feet on concrete, in the seismic collision
of shoulders and hips lunging for the try line, or the throng & buzz
of bees and wasps among long grass and thin weeds; or sticky lips
locked on lips in the secret space beneath houses. Boys have no
business with god

until their bodies lengthen and sin begins to stick to their tongues.

Soon after, our weekly hajj halted. Our family became families
and rupture became familiar. In this, metaphor & Middle East are
one. In the long months away from that imagined country, I heard
of an older cousin, a name hushed by others, a man in love with
men, and in his absence I saw my future: who knew you could
ghost the living?

Who knew you could bury the ghetto in forgetting?

I am unearthing yesterday, ungathering this bouquet of quiet,
reappearing in inches. Lebanon was left incomplete in Warwick
Farm, & everywhere else we went, the ragged tops of mountains
peeking out of windows; the Sacred House in fragments, in
bloodied bits of stone, in black and gold petals on the floor.
Though the builders are gone,

they left the blueprints in my skin, every alley & every river,
every ghost & every ghetto.

Omar Sakr

**The Kaaba is a building at the centre of Islam's most holy mosque Al-Masjid
Al-Haram, in Mecca. It is the building all Muslims pray towards, and to which they
must journey at least once in their lifetime, which is called the hajj. The Kaaba has
many names, including Sacred House, House of Allah, House of God in Heaven, etc.*

*** As part of the hajj, Muslims perform a ritual known as the Stoning of the Devil,
in which they throw stones at three pillars known as al-jamarāt.*

Hossegor

Surfing probably didn't occur to the Vikings
    but then you never know—maybe one of Asgeir's men
      found himself oaring his chieftain's faering

for this Biscay shore, just as a set wave jacked—
    the kind that narrows the eyes of the guns
      who yearly light up the Quicksilver Pro

(Slater, Fanning, Medina, Florence, Parko)—
    and intuiting to lean down the face of the monster
      felt it take, the shove as the hull slotted flush

into the vein of the sea god, frisson pitching through
    the crew like the shudder of a brained seal
      as they fluked the drop on an outside bomb.

You can almost see them now, rolling in from
    out the back like hoons on a banana boat,
      on course to plow through locals. A nerf howls

to a thud; a kitesurfer eats it. And there must
    have been some among the numberless wrecked
      who happened to cling to jetsam felicitously warped—

the waterlogged panel of a walnut armoire, say—
    as to hitch them a lift in the home stretch
      of this crumbling A-frame's deep Atlantic fetch.

Perhaps one of them even cottoned on
    that after breathing, the art lies in the reading
      of the break, getting to grips with tide-shift

and how the wind's caprice vexes the takeoff,
    the fickle line-up—but who among them
        could have envisaged a Tahitian king, carving?

The guns will return, who are now braving
    the skull-crushing torque of Teahupo'o.

Jaya Savige

The body

The body has many duties. Lust
Is only one of them. Though it is close to hand
We learn the extent of things through the body.

Strange, then. That we are so constricted.
What we thought everything proves to be nothing.
Constriction is the only lesson we carry.

When we are young everything seems possible,
Even flight, but soon enough we are contained
Within the practical centre of our bodies.

So that, in old age, all limitations seem natural.
It is as if the body always held us,
A natural constriction to our widest dreams.

These days I think I am confined
Or at least held back from everything
As if what I dreamed were ever possible.

Thomas Shapcott

Around the World

Sydney, sixteen and a half, I took part
in a chess tournament called the Riga Shield,
knowing nothing then of that fabled city.
Byzantium too was yet to traverse my page,
like poetry, and Prague remained
a train-station where we had waited for hours,
in a wagon from Warsaw to Vienna,
for something that would arrive soon enough—
my first climb above the gorgeous clouds
of the Mediterranean behind a Convair
cabin window, front row, portside, right behind
the flight deck's forbidden musics.
I did know something of the Baltic states
(Soviet Republics then), from *Around the World*:
some of its pictures brought me the shock
of the real, especially the chapterette 'IRAN'—
brown print of two blindfolded figures
each strung slumped to a pole, labelled in Polish
'Bestial execution of democrats sentenced
by the shah's regime'. It sat opposite
a sample stamp and the silhouetted little map
of the country in question dark within its diagram
continent. I treasure that book, although
now of course I know: little changes—
in some places you can hang for mixing metaphors.
I was happy to mix chess with geography, both
I grew to love. They somehow seemed

to complement each other—and me, in my
consequential otherness. These days we're cajoled
into splitting our differences, it wasn't always
thus. But as I skimmed 1965, new skies
unfolding before me, sixteen and a half, that chess
of becoming (my games all zealously notated),
I too was balancing the difference—
between where I had been or never been,
and whatever I couldn't know I was waiting for.

Alex Skovron

Argument

A poem addressed to Elizabeth Bishop

My husband and I were well south of your temperate Brazil.
We were bunkered in a valley where a glacier, groaning
    with the debris of ages and all its splintering wrecks,
    had abruptly dammed itself.
That frozen monument clogged the lake outside our hotel,
    where the gales slaughtered the rocks on the shore and
    roughed the crooked trees into brooms.
This was no place for romance.
Even the birds and insects knew it,
    the sky and earth blown of traffic.
Time, though, was everywhere.
Outside our hotel room, three icebergs—calved from the glacier
    —sat mammoth on the chopped water,
    age-old and dumb.
I don't remember the trigger: only that the trap snapped and I
    was sprung.
(It had never mattered where in the world I ran.)
As always, I dragged down the closest man.
The day wore inexorably on and on, until the weight of the moon
    and stars was spilling gravel and filling
    the cold hole we were in.

There was nothing *gentle*, as you described it,
    about the battleground of reason's end.
Days later my husband and I were slumped on a cruiser
    designed for viewing all the postures of ancient ice
    re-birthed by the radioactive sun.
Quelled of motion sickness, we could barely keep our eyes open.
Meanwhile the other passengers shifted like a tide
    from their seats to the deck each time the boat slowed

alongside some blue-faced mutant from history.
Cameras clicked as if there was no tomorrow.
In truth, it was hard to believe in a future.
The tour guide, though, had no time for pathos:
    her electrified voice reckoned with us
    in one language, then another, and still another.
We drowsed, cold shoulder to shoulder, with nothing to say,
    held afloat in that science-fiction Babel.
What will buoy us now, I wonder, as I sit alone in our car,
    years later, on a suburban night,
        ignoring the tender offering of the porch light?
Now that death looms large, ready to calve, just for the two of us.

Maria Takolander

Jakhan Pollyeva

Putin's speechwriter in a leopard print dress
with plunging neckline performs her latest poems
before chatting up the President of Kyrgyzstan.
Her heels are higher than most poets wear them.
There are people like this in every palace
of either sex and any age. Each of them
has a following. They are the singers
Ulysses heard, the Loreleis, the stars.

She wears too much lipstick but she bought
her blondness somewhere no-one reading this
could afford. She has for long
been promoted way beyond speechwriter,
is described as "aide". The future of millions
depends on her stylist and on
the literary critics, which amounts
to the same thing. Those of us who prefer
other voices, other ways of phrasing
sweet evil remember interrogation
and shut up.

         At literary events
I try to learn acceptable applause.
Old football commentators say,
"If you wear white boots you'd better kick goals."

Tim Thorne

Young Folly

It must seem like a mountain of folly
to the old people, but we take our chances
and we're always on the ready.

We're on the ready, right now, and yet
they think we're just a troubled handful
of trouble, just can't go straight,

can't go straight like the arrow of time
that speeds from ancient times to right now
to get you between the eyes. This is the realm

behind the eyes, with its whip-quick
answers to how to behave, its cheap vow
to be better, much better, quickly broken

so that what is not better is boarding
at boarding time, those giant flying machines.
We take a drag, and fuck the lung.

Fuck the drag of the air, the horizon's curve.
We're all going on a summer holiday, already gone
into sad age waiting, with just a wave.

John Tranter

Note: 'Young Folly' began as a draft using the end-words of 'The Young'
by Roddy Lumsden. *The Open Door*, page 24.

Invisible Spears

A stadium can hold the most sound
drowning out the bora ring
mudding the lines we needed to know
where we're going
now it's a clusterfuck to get the train home
flip up seats and overflowing beer
the rude odour of tomato sauce
and the black faces they never show on TV
the team with the most blackfullas
they don't want to win
the commentator's curse
the tiddling fear
of invisible spears
we can't score goals
on this sacred land
celebrated as animals
GI doing the goanna, yeah
but not people
with military intelligence
you don't want us protecting
our land like the Maori
– that means it was our land to protect
we don't need
a haka of whitefullas
just let us resist.

Ellen van Neerven

An Object exists only as it might exist to Another

The melancholia of not being Anne Boyer.
The melancholia of melancholy,
of listening for factories out there in the sea
when everyone else was searching for whales.
The melancholia of a word without a poem,
of the poem as pristine category looking forwards
to an unseasonable year. The melancholia
of mid-size body suits still wrapped in the box.
The melancholia of the test subject
reduced to running slip or outmoded art form.
The melancholia of the barely perceptible
snakeskin purse clutched on breezy afternoons
of laissez-faire capitalism. It's true, isn't it?
Only the romantic can be that real.
The melancholia of sharp, leopard-print belts
burning naively at the fashion blog
found in the heart of yesteryear.
The melancholia of the human
as a class of actors, reciting *Moby Dick*
to the signature tunes of Prince. The melancholia
of melancholy, writing city rather than cosmos.
The melancholia of repetition,
recidivist as the eye that refuses
to gaze back at you. One woman's fantasy
is another's solipsism.
The melancholia of not being loved,
firstly in the age of Aquarius and then again
in the age of the Anthropocene.
Or the melancholia of window dressing
the incision between innocence and experience.

Ann Vickery

Altogether Elsewhere

(Auden's hundred-plus)

Your first words that I read were "Look, stranger,"
    which really stuck.
You hymned environmental danger
and illness welling up from bottled anger
    in the out-of-luck.

Stranger than any of us was your
    thanatology:
mental mapping was a chart of war
but lust for a diagonal metaphor
    fed your geology.

Ominous uniforms and the sexy furs
    you parsed as threat
like acid rain in silted aquifers
the Romans left. From gaunt commissioners
    an each-way bet

gave your calciferous frontier the chance
    either of Left or Right.
You didn't much approve of France,
for their symbolist poetic dance
    was a downright

draught of colourless Coca-Cola,
    not for grown-ups,
a canker in the thinker's molar.
You could have liked Savonarola,
    but in his cups.

You'd have known the date of each bubonic
        outbreak, or heresy;
you knew that most blokes are moronic
and your blow-job poem was merely platonic –
        well, ostensibly.

Ambiguous Europe has its weather still:
        expert in exile
you turned the twilight into chlorophyll
soodling along beside the sacred rill
        mile after lucky mile.

Chris Wallace-Crabbe

A Plein-Air Artist Reflects on Timing

It was a cool summer afternoon.
White-plumed honeyeaters worked quickly,
gathering insects from the leaves of a gum.
A plane swept low in laps for a parade.

I noticed how the fences of my garden
stood by idly. I thought, someday if I
could watch this scene afresh, caught on film –
a given light, the given earth, and me,
here, but held by time at one remove –
then all reserve would vanish.
I would grasp each detail keenly.

Alas my thoughts turned to a nerve in my back,
to the undue fame of my enemies, and to my future
glory – majestic as the ocean
meeting the shore. I have recorded nothing.

Simon West

On This

Coming at you like a wave its wide scoop full of surfers
the threat of marriage. The wedding band
will encircle you softly as the sea
laps all around an island.

You won't even want to swim to the headland.
All the world and all its work cry to you
this is the thing,
and once you have pegged down a gentleman
who might otherwise billow like a kite
in the endless green
lubbery sky of himself
once you have got him and he has got you.

Sapphires glancing in the foam.
Suitors surge in on tall ships.
Penelope weaves and unweaves for the one
above all others.
How he flowers in the mind like a wild transparent violet
held to sunlit glass.

Petra White

FAUNE et JEUX

I thought that gold was harder than paper,
but paper turned out to be harder

                    – Vaslav Nijinsky

<u>Prelude</u>

A wicked ball, a fluent veil—
    dance itself   the object of desire
not the one who wields or wears.

So many eyes—it is the war
              and time is out of joint
with ink—   *everywhere*

the notebook keeps on   sliding;
   all shapes and beauty fluid
as the fountain pen unleashed.

This door is never locked
   though people are afraid to say:
I do not understand—but *feel*.

<u>I. *L'Après midi d'un faune*</u>

   My madness is my love towards mankind
                     – Vaslav Nijinsky

Mischievous sanctuary—withdrawn
   into the score   *alive!*

            another crime:
the faun is me—

              it's all in the choreography
          grinding the pastoral air

              two flattened hooves in profile
                              blades

This is my body: piebald   on a mound
    quietly, grapes

                  one bunch
                        two   is all you do—

delight in slow time   tease
                              a fire in the narrow green

              of Bakst's impression—
                    need for nothing else.

              *

A distraction: nymphets on the incline
                 fleet-footed arms wide open
                 crossing flat space like so many lines of poetry
                                        three
                        two
          one   rouged by the stream imaginary

The faun is I—control
                    oh   head thrown back
              the teeth bared   hideous
                    the ears pricked

your lost children, easily spooked by the eye in my forehead.
I know the true beast
                    Ah! Ah! is not horror but <u>joy</u>

They think I am funny
                    unhook my arm and *run!*

The goat in me will eat the veil   lick it
                                      push it to the mound
                                      grinding

Know this:
                    my instrument   though roundly hissed
                        will whistle life into the vase
                            as an outpouring of encore flowers

<u>II. Jeux</u>

>   His cruel and barbarous choreography
>   trampled all over my poor rhythms
>   like so many weeds
>   – Claude Debussy

I have a secret to share with you:
    a ball thrown astray
    in the garden   at dusk
    is how people come together, even
    if we cannot recall
            contact   fault   love
            sidelined for a flirt

                ~ twentieth-century triple kiss;
                ~ a Zepplin or an aeroplane disaster
                ~ the tango and the turkey trot

    all my ideas, rejected.

I want pointes in the court—
    back and forth, a three-way match,
    weird trajectories!

Grip my handle for a deuce *pas de* pout ⎫
                                   ⎬ fit with technique
Now you—grip my handle *pas de* pout ⎭ and 60 tempo markings

Observe the working of my brain
    as I butt you in the stomach   and then you, too!

It's a two ball dance and the rhythm is fierce
    enough to knock you up

                              stage
      match, set, game:

The crowd turned *wild*.

Curtain call

          Jerky handwriting means kindness of heart.
      He is a bad man.
My trunks are packed.
A cure for cancer and a new pen.

I do not reason in the theatre square.
I am a pupil of the round
      and round I go—the dance as life
         the life as fun and games   "mere delusions"

  Oh   now the blood has rushed to my head and down I fall
                easy prey for beasts
                in Zurich's withered garden.

Well: I will stalk your faux propriety—hoof
          at your iron closets with my short tail wagging.

I am the faun, and *Jeux* is incomplete.

Elusive game!—
               I know what earth is
          even if the steps are gone.
          One giant leap across that stream
          could prove the skill in an idea—a dream
                    of thrusting forward, somehow.

          But   what kind of leap to court
                              with the wings, closing in?

     (some thought)
               silent, *san rigueur*:

                         return to the mound
                         remove the circlet
                         discard the veil
               Ah.
                    Ah.

          Wild joy is in the brown study
          where the faun will take his leave
          fold inwards
          and sleep, *peacefully.*

          Sleep, sleep peacefully.

Jessica L. Wilkinson

Poppies, Katoomba

I didn't come here to write poems about flowers
but there are poppies of palest purple.
Blown open, each petal
cup-shaped, like an empty hand and
every time I travel my chest winds tight:
what kind of creature
cannot take a holiday? In a hotel bar,
I chance upon an old friend of my father
nibbling on scones, he says that as a child
I'd said *I want to be alone*
with my own thoughts and this winds me,
although I can't say why. The poppies
are membranous, the poppies are
precarious, the poppies
are bruise-coloured at their centre.
By the time I get the poppies
to my desk
they are bedraggled,
their hard, green hearts
all they have left to show me.

Fiona Wright

Self Publishing

In a way, everything is self publishing. When you open your
mouth to talk, you are self publishing because you don't want
someone else to speak for you even if he or she were the
speech writer for Howard or Bush or Mao Zedong. When the
rain decides to fall it is self publishing, on a regional scale,
sometimes on a statewide scale. You can't dismiss it as unworthily
self publishing because it doesn't fall on a national scale or
international scale. Rivers in the world are self publishing on
a daily and nightly basis. Even a little creek is self publishing
when it winds its way through an industrial zone clogged with
toxicity and waste. Birds never remain quiet because they don't
get paid for calling, their ways of self publishing that are never
actually recorded in human history, not even in birds' history,
and when sometimes it does get recorded as in relaxation music
they still don't get paid and they still keep singing, their ways
of self publishing. Some great self publishers include James
Joyce Marcel Proust Anais Nin Margaret Atwood William
Blake Virginia Woolf D.H. Lawrence Walter Whitman Mark
Twain Lord Byron Percy Bysshe Shelley Ouyang and Yu, even
Benjamin Britten had to found English Opera Group in 1947
and the Aldeburgh Festival in 1948 "partly (though not solely)
to perform his own works" (See http://en.wikipedia.org/wiki/
Benjamin_Britten). That's self publishing. If self publishing
is a crime, issue proceedings against us and take us all to an
international court where the presiding judge is a well-published
and award-winning author who has never self published (Shame
on Him!) and will sentence us all to a lifetime imprisonment of
self publishers and a deathtime of self publishers

Now listen, to the rain self publishing again as it did 3000
million years ago, on the page that is my roof

Ouyang Yu

{180}

Boat Song

Speed, bonnie boat, like a bird on the wing,
'Onward', the seekers cry;
Speed, you will not, but sink like a stone
Down on the seabed lie.

'We once had a country', the desperate cry
'Now we're officially dead'.
The Ministers grin, 'You cannot come in.
You'd consume all our daily bread'.

The debris of massacres, blitzkriegs and bombings,
Putsches and pogroms, war's goings and comings.
Tyres are for burning and cobbles for throwing,
Army surplus for wearing and weeds fit for mowing.

Lie in military tents with fear gripping breath,
Forget that you're living, expecting a death.
Remote ideologies send bonnie boats
Like broken-winged birds to our merciful votes.

And we turned them away, yes, we turned them away
As we went out to play
In our dead-hearted country, the bounteous place
Where neighbourly love puts a smile on each face.

As we golf and we gamble, eat, make love and die,
Raise shrines to our roadkill, release a brief sigh—
Only heaven knows why—and for hours upon hours
We bring photos and candles and
Mountains of flowers upon flowers upon
Flowers upon flowers

Fay Zwicky

One Last Poem

I was going to write one last poem
but nothing came out,
only lightning & red sand
& a campfire that speaks
at least fifteen Aboriginal dialects
as it stirs the embers with a stick.
Even a whitefella can understand
two or three sentences
if he's prepared to press
his ear to the flames.
The Pintupi have forgotten more than
I'll ever know about the Land –
its ways & names.
Too much to remember,
other than the warning:
don't eat *kuka* in the rain.
"Proper cheeky bugger, lightning."

Today a friend told me,
"everything's a metaphor for something else."
But what I don't understand is:
why, when I wanted to describe you, was
the only metaphor that came to mind
the sound of wind blowing in from the desert?

Billy Marshall Stoneking

Publication Details

All the poems that do not appear below were previously unpublished

Martin Harrison's 'Patio' appeared in his collection *Happiness*, (UWAP, July 2015).

Adam Aitken's 'In The Billy Sing Baghdad Bar-and-Grill' appeared in *Peril: Asian–Australian Arts and Culture*, June 2016 (online).

Jordie Albiston's '∟' appeared in the *Journal of Humanistic Mathematics*, vol. 6.1, January 2016 (USA).

Chris Andrew's 'Advanced Souvlaki' appeared in *Southerly*, vol. 75, no. 2, February 2016.

Evelyn Araluen's 'Learning Bundjalung on Tharawal' appeared in *Overland*, vol. 223, Winter 2016.

Ken Bolton's 'Dark Heart' appeared in the *Cordite Poetry Review*, 1 February 2016.

Peter Boyle's 'Discovered in a rock pool' appeared in the *Cordite Poetry Review*, 1 November 2015.

Michael Brennan's 'There and Then' appeared in *Poetry* 208.2, May 2016.

Lisa Brockwell's 'Waiting on Imran Khan' appeared in *Poetry* 208.2, May 2016.

Kevin Brophy's 'Siren' appeared in *Australian Book Review's Victorian States of Poetry anthology (2016)*.

Lachlan Brown's 'Suspended Belief' appeared in *Underneath: the University of Canberra Vice-Chancellor's International Poetry Prize 2015*, edited by Owen Bullock and Niloofar Fanaiyan (Axon Elements, 2015).

Pam Brown's 'Rooibos' appeared in the *Hunter Anthology of Contemporary Australian Feminist Poetry*, edited by Jessica L. Wilkinson and Bonny Cassidy (Hunter Publishers, 2016).

Michelle Cahill's 'Car Lover' appeared in the *Hunter Anthology of Contemporary Australian Feminist Poetry*, edited by Jessica L. Wilkinson and Bonny Cassidy (Hunter Publishers, 2016).

Elizabeth Campbell's 'Cloaca Maxima' appeared in *Poetry* 208.2, May 2016.

Bonny Cassidy's 'Axe derby' appeared in *Poetry* 208.2, May 2016.

Julie Chevalier's 'Plan B' appeared in *Meanjin*, vol. 75, no. 1, Autumn 2016.

Eileen Chong's 'Magnolia' appeared in *Meanjin*, vol. 75, no. 1, Autumn 2016.

Aidan Coleman's 'Secondary' appeared in *Australian Book Review's South Australian States of Poetry anthology (2016)*.

Stuart Cooke's 'Hinterland' appeared in *Contra Equus Niveus*, vol. 3 (USA, 2016).

MTC Cronin's 'ABOVE US' appeared in *Australian Book Review's Queensland States of Poetry anthology (2016)*.

Nathan Curnow's 'Swimming (my lane)' appeared in *PRISM International*, vol. 54, no. 1, September 2015.

Luke Davies' 'Heisenberg Saying Goodbye to Mum at Lilyfield' appeared in Poetry 208.2, May 2016.

Sarah Day's 'Wooden Horse' appeared in *Underneath: The University of Canberra Vice-Chancellor's International Poetry Prize 2015*, edited by Owen Bullock and Niloofar Fanaiyan (Axon Elements, 2015).

Joel Deane's 'Following the many elbows of the Yarra' appeared in *Australian Book Review*, 21 January 2016.

Jelena Dinic's 'The Silence of Siskins' appeared in *Australian Book Review's South Australian States of Poetry anthology (2016)*.

Dan Disney's 'Untitled: villaknelle xvi' appeared in his collection *either, Orpheus* (UWAP, 2016).

Lucy Dougan's 'Right Through Me' appeared in her collection *The Guardians* (Giramondo, 2015).

Laurie Duggan's 'A northern winter' appeared in *Cordite Poetry Review*, 1 February 2016.

Ali Cobby Eckermann's 'Black Deaths in Custody' appeared in *Poetry* 208.2, May 2016.

Stephen Edgar's 'Hearts and Minds' appeared in *Australian Poetry Journal*, vol. 6, no. 1, June 2016.

Anne Elvey's 'working from home – to do list' appeared in *Cordite Poetry Review*, 1 November 2015.

Michael Farrell's 'Death of a Year' appeared in *Plumwood Mountain*, vol. 2, no.2, September 2015.

Liam Ferney's 'Requiem' appeared in *Island*, no. 145, 2016.

Toby Fitch's 'Janus' appeared in *Australian Poetry Anthology 2015*, edited by Brook Emery and Sarah Holland-Batt (Australian Poetry, 2015).

Lionel G. Fogarty's 'Ambition Man' appeared in *Australian Book Review's Queensland States of Poetry anthology (2016)*.

Tina Giannoukos' 'XXXI' appeared in her collection *Bull Days* (ASP/Arcadia, 2016).

Robert Gray's 'The Latter Days' appeared in the *Australian REVIEW*, 20 February 2016.

Phillip Hall's 'Royalty' appeared in *Plumwood Mountain*, vol. 2, no.2, September 2015.

Natalie Harkin's 'Cultural Precinct' appeared in *Cordite Poetry Review*, 1 February 2016.

Dennis Haskell's 'Tinnitus' appeared in his collection *Ahead of Us* (Fremantle Press, 2016).

Dominique Hecq's 'Archive Fever' appeared in *Axon*, issue 9, 2016.

Paul Hetherington's 'Black Dress' appeared in *Australian Book Review's ACT States of Poetry anthology (2016)*.

Fiona Hile's 'Relocation of the Big Prawn' appeared in *Axon*, issue 10, 2016.

Andy Jackson's 'The change room' appeared in *Cordite Poetry Review*, 4 May 2016.

Lisa Jacobson's 'The Jews of Hamburg Speak Out' appeared in *Writing to the Wire*, edited by Dan Disney and Kit Kelen (UWAP, 2016).

Virginia Jealous' 'First contact, Kakadu' appeared in the *Weekend Australian*, 11 June 2016.

A. Frances Johnson's 'Diary of an Anti-elegist' appeared in *Australian Book Review's Victorian States of Poetry anthology (2016)*.

Jill Jones' 'In Flight Entertainment' appeared in *Cordite Poetry Review*, 1 February 2016.

Kit Kelen's 'takk for alt' appeared in *Cordite Poetry Review*, 1 February 2016.

Cate Kennedy's 'Limbo' appeared in *Prayers of a Secular World*, edited by Jordie Albiston and Kevin Brophy (Inkerman & Blunt, 2015).

John Kinsella's 'Spatial Realignment of Jam Tree Gully' appeared in the *Australian Book Review*, October 2015.

Andy Kissane's 'Getting away with it' appeared in the *Weekend Australian REVIEW*, 24 October 2015.

Shari Kocher's 'Foxstruck' appeared in the *Australian Poetry Journal*, vol. 5, issue 2, November 2015.

Simeon Kronenberg's 'Bringing It All Back Home' appeared in *Meanjin*, vol. 75, no. 1, Autumn 2016.

Verity Laughton's 'Kangarilla, Summer, 2016' appeared in *Australian Book Review*, no. 380, April 2016.

Anthony Lawrence's 'Wax Cathedral' appeared in his collection *Headwaters* (Pitt Street Poetry, 2016).

Bronwyn Lea's 'Blow Job (kama sutra)' appeared in *Island*, no.144 (2016).

Kate Lilley's 'Lovestore' appeared in *Cordite Poetry Review*, 1 February 2016.

Kate Llewellyn's 'Possibly' appeared in *Australian Book Review's South Australian States of Poetry anthology (2016)*.

Cameron Lowe's 'Pastoral/"Asset Management"' appeared in *Australian Book Review's Victorian States of Poetry anthology (2016)*.

Jennifer Maiden's 'Orchards' appeared in her collection *The Fox Petition* (Giramondo, 2015).

Caitlin Maling's 'Intimacy' appeared in *Island*, no. 145 (2016).

David Malouf's 'Visitation on Myrtle Street' appeared in *Australian Book Review*, 15 April 2016.

Kate Middleton's 'Study of a Lion' appeared in *Australian Book Review's NSW States of Poetry anthology (2016)*.

Peter Minter's 'Craft' appeared in *Meanjin*, vol. 75, no. 1, 15 June 2016.

Les Murray's 'Nuclear Family Bees' appeared in his collection *Waiting for the Past* (Black Inc, 2015).

π.o.'s 'Shakespeare & the State Library' appeared in *Fitzroy: The Biography* (Collective Effort Press, 2015).

Ella O'Keefe's 'Letter from the swimming pool' appeared in *Active Aesthetics: Contemporary Australian Poetry*, edited by Daniel Benjamin and Claire Marie Stancek (Giramondo, 2016).

Meredi Ortega's 'Cyborg Me' appeared in the *Hunter Anthology of Contemporary Australian Feminist Poetry*, edited by Jessica L. Wilkinson and Bonny Cassidy (Hunter Publishers, 2016).

Geoff Page's 'Ekphrasis' appeared in the *Australian*, 20 February 2016.

Charmaine Papertalk-Green & John Kinsella's *from* 'Hawes – God's Intruder' appeared in *Southerly*, vol. 75, no. 2, February 2016.

Felicity Plunkett's '"A Decidedly Pathological Process:' appeared in the *Hunter Anthology of Contemporary Australian Feminist Poetry*, edited by Jessica L. Wilkinson and Bonny Cassidy (Hunter Publishers, 2016).

Hessom Razavi's 'Shabnam Nightwish' appeared in the *Hunter Anthology of Contemporary Australian Feminist Poetry*, edited by Jessica L. Wilkinson and Bonny Cassidy (Hunter Publishers, 2016).

Peter Rose's 'The Subject of Feeling' appeared in his collection *The Subject of Feeling* (UWAP, 2015).

Robyn Rowland's 'Night Watch' appeared in *Falling and Flying: Poems on Ageing*, edited by Judith Beveridge and Dr Sue Ogle (Brandl & Schlesinger, 2015).

Gig Ryan's 'Astronomical Twilight' appeared in *Cordite Poetry Review*, 4 May 2016.

Thomas Shapcott's 'The body' appeared in the *Age*, 9 July 2016.

Alex Skovron's 'Around the World' appeared in the *Australian Poetry Anthology 2015*, edited by Brook Emery and Sarah Holland-Batt (Australian Poetry, 2015).

John Tranter's 'Young Folly' appeared in *Overland*, vol. 220, Spring 2015.

Ellen van Neervan's 'Invisible Spears' appeared in *Overland*, vol. 220, Spring 2015.

Chris Wallace-Crabbe's 'Altogether Elsewhere' appeared in *Cordite Poetry Review*, 1 October 2015.

Simon West's 'A Plein-Air Artist Reflects on Timing' appeared in the *Sydney Morning Herald*, 19 November 2015.

Petra White's 'On This' appeared in *Writing to the Wire*, edited by Dan Disney and Kit Kelen (UWAP, 2016).

Jessica L. Wilkinson's 'FAUNE et JEUX' appeared in *Australian Book Review's Victorian States of Poetry anthology (2016)*.

Ouyang Yu's 'Self Publishing' appeared in his collection *Fainting with Freedom* (Five Islands Press, 2015).

Fay Zwicky's 'Boat Song' appeared in *Writing to the Wire*, edited by Dan Disney and Kit Kelen (UWAP, 2016).

Billy Marshall Stoneking's 'One Last Poem' appeared in *Transnational Literature*, vol. 8.1, Nov 2015.

Notes on Contributors

THE EDITOR

Sarah Holland-Batt is an award-winning poet, critic, editor and academic. She is the recipient of fellowships from Yaddo and MacDowell colonies in the United States, the Marten Bequest Travelling Scholarship, an Asialink Literature Residency, and the Australia Council Literature Residency at the B.R. Whiting Studio in Rome, among other honours. She was educated at the University of Queensland and New York University, where she was the 2010 W.G. Walker Memorial Fulbright Scholar. Her most recent book of poems, *The Hazards* (UQP), was shortlisted for the New South Wales Premier's Kenneth Slessor Prize, the AFAL John Bray Memorial Poetry Award, the Queensland Literary Awards Judith Wright Calanthe Award, and the Western Australian Premier's Book Awards. She presently lives in Brisbane, where she works as a Senior Lecturer in Creative Writing at QUT, and the poetry editor of *Island*.

POETS

Martin Harrison was an Australian poet and essayist. He worked at the ABC as a producer and broadcaster. For many years Martin taught writing and sound studies at the University of Technology in Sydney. The hundreds of students he mentored into successful writing careers constitute part of his legacy. Martin died in September 2014.

Robert Adamson's latest collection, *Net Needle* (Black Inc., 2015), was shortlisted for the Judith Wright Calanthe Award in the Queensland Premier's Literary Awards. *The Golden Bird* (Black Inc., 2009) won the C.J. Dennis Prize for Poetry in the 2009 Victorian Premier's Literary Awards. *The Goldfinches of Baghdad* (Flood, 2006) won the *Age* Book of the Year Award for poetry and was shortlisted for the NSW and Queensland premiers' awards.

Adam Aitken is the author of four full-length collections of poetry and co-edited *Contemporary Asian Australian Poets* (Puncher & Wattmann, 2013). His most recent poetry and essays have appeared in *Southerly*, *Axon* and *Transnational Literature*. His memoir, *One Hundred Letters Home* (Vagabond Press), was published in 2016.

Jordie Albiston has published nine poetry collections and a handbook on poetic form. Jordie possesses an ongoing pre-occupation with mathematical constructs and constraints, and the possibilities offered in terms of poetic structure. Her work has won many awards, including the Mary Gilmore Award and the 2010 NSW Premier's Award. She lives in Melbourne.

Chris Andrews teaches at Western Sydney University. He has published two collections of poems: *Cut Lunch* (Indigo, 2002) and *Lime Green Chair* (Waywiser, 2012). He has also translated books of Latin American fiction, including *Ema: César Aira the Captive* (New Directions, 2016).

Evelyn Araluen is a PhD candidate and educator working with Indigenous literatures at the University of Sydney, and a founding member of Students Support Aboriginal Communities, a NSW grassroots activist network. Her father's ancestors are Bundjalung, and her mother's Wiradjuri. She lives between Dharug and Eora country.

Judith Beveridge is the author of six collections of poetry, most recently *Devadatta's Poems* (Giramondo, 2014), which was shortlisted for the NSW and Queensland premiers' poetry prizes and the Prime Minister's Poetry Award. Her new and selected poems will appear in 2017.

Ken Bolton is a poet, art critic, editor and publisher. Originally from Sydney, he has lived in Adelaide since 1982. 'Dark Heart' was the name of a not very good exhibition at the Art Gallery of South Australia, in 2014. The version of 'You're My Thrill' is by Pepper Adams.

Peter Boyle was born in Melbourne but has lived most of his life in Sydney. He has seven collections of poetry, most recently *Ghostspeaking* (Vagabond Press, 2016), *Towns in the Great Desert* (Puncher & Wattmann, 2013) and *Apocrypha* (Vagabond Press, 2009). He has translated poetry extensively from French and Spanish.

Michael Brennan is an Australian writer based in Tokyo, Japan. His books include *The Imageless World* (Salt Publishing, 2003), *Unanimous Night* (Salt Publishing, 2008) and *Autoethnographic* (Giramondo, 2012). Since 1999, he has run Vagabond Press (www. vagabondpress.net).

Lisa Brockwell lives on a rural property near Byron Bay, Australia, with her husband and young son. She was runner-up in the University of Canberra Vice-Chancellor's International Poetry Prize in 2015. Her first collection, *Earth Girls*, was published in 2016 by Pitt Street Poetry.

David Brooks' most recent publications are *Open House* (poetry: UQP, 2015), *Napoleon's Roads* (short fiction: UQP, 2015) and *Derrida's Breakfast* (essays: Brandl & Schlesinger, 2016). An Honorary Associate Professor at the University of Sydney, he is co-editor of *Southerly* and the 2015/16 Australia Council Fellow in Fiction.

Kevin Brophy is the author of fourteen books of fiction, poetry and essays, including *This is What Gives Us Time* (Gloria SMH Press, 2016). In 2015 he was poet in residence at the B.R. Whiting Studio in Rome. He teaches Creative Writing at the University of Melbourne.

Lachlan Brown grew up in Macquarie Fields, Sydney. He currently teaches and researches at Charles Sturt University in Wagga Wagga. Lachlan's first book of poetry, *Limited Cities* (Giramondo, 2012), was highly commended for the Mary Gilmore Award. His second volume of poetry (forthcoming in 2017) explores aspects of his Chinese/ Australian heritage.

Pam Brown has been active in many ventures in the multitudinous and continually shifting zone of Australian poetry and in other cultural scenes for over four decades. She is a contributing editor for several magazines and independent publishers. Her eighteenth book, *Missing up*, was published by Vagabond Press in 2015.

Joanne Burns' most recent poetry collection is *brush* (Giramondo, 2014), the winner of the 2016 NSW Premier's Literary Awards Kenneth Slessor Poetry Prize. She is currently assembling a selected volume of her work called *real land*, spanning over four decades of book and journal publication. She lives in Sydney.

Michelle Cahill is an award-winning poet and fiction author. Her recent books are *Letter to Pessoa* (Giramondo, 2016), *Night Birds* (Vagabond Press, 2014) and *Vishvarupa* (Five Islands Press, 2011), which was shortlisted in the Victorian Premier's Literary Awards. Her poems and essays have appeared in *Island*, the *Weekend Australian* and *Sydney Review of Books*.

Elizabeth Campbell was born in Melbourne in 1980. She has been the recipient of many prizes, including the Vincent Buckley Prize, the Marten Bequest Travelling Scholarship and an Australia Council residency in Rome. Her books, *Letters To The Tremulous Hand* (2007) and *Error* (2011), are published by John Leonard Press.

Bonny Cassidy's most recent book is *Final Theory* (Giramondo, 2014). She is Feature Reviews Editor for *Cordite Poetry Review*, and, with Jessica L. Wilkinson, co-edited *Contemporary Australian Feminist Poetry* (Hunter Publishers, 2016). Bonny lectures in Creative Writing at RMIT University.

Julie Chevalier writes poetry and short fiction in Sydney. Her second poetry collection, *Darger: his girls* (Puncher & Wattmann, 2012), was awarded the Alec Bolton Prize for an Unpublished Poetry Manuscript, and shortlisted for the WA Premier's Poetry Prize. *Permission to Lie*, a short story collection, was published by Spineless Wonders in 2011.

Eileen Chong is a Sydney poet. Her books are *Burning Rice* (2012), *Peony* (2014) and *Painting Red Orchids* (2016), all from Pitt Street Poetry. Her work has been shortlisted for the Prime Minister's Literary Awards, the Anne Elder Award and the Peter Porter Poetry Prize, amongst others. *Another Language* is forthcoming with George Braziller in New York City in Spring 2017.

Aidan Coleman lives in Adelaide. His two collections of poetry have been shortlisted for the NSW Premier's Kenneth Slessor Prize, the Adelaide Festival Awards for Literature and the Western Australian Premier's Book Awards. He also writes reviews, speeches and Shakespeare textbooks.

Stuart Cooke is a poet and critic based on the Gold Coast, where he lectures at Griffith University. His books include *Opera* (Five Islands Press, 2016), *George Dyuŋgayan's Bulu Line: A West Kimberley Song Cycle* (Puncher & Wattman, 2014) and *Edge Music* (Vagabond Press, 2011).

MTC Cronin has published twenty books (poetry, prose poems and essays). Recent collections include *In Possession of Loss* (Shearsman Books, 2014) and *The Law of Poetry* (Puncher & Wattmann, 2015), the latter of which was written over two decades.

Nathan Curnow is a past editor of *Going Down Swinging*. His previous books include *The Ghost Poetry Project* (Puncher & Wattmann, 2009), *RADAR* (Walleah Press, 2012) and *The Right Wrong Notes* (Macau ASM, 2015). His most recent collection, *The Apocalypse Awards* (ASP, 2016), is inspired by the absurdity of the modern world and charts our collective obsession with the end times.

Luke Davies is a poet, novelist and screenwriter. His *Interferon Psalms* (Allen & Unwin, 2011) won the inaugural Prime Minister's Award for Poetry. His other books include *Running With Light* (Allen & Unwin, 1999) and *Totem* (Allen & Unwin, 2004). The film of his novel *Candy* (Ballantine Books, 1997), from which Davies adapted his own screenplay, starred the late Heath Ledger. His film *Lion* premiered at the Toronto Film Festival.

Sarah Day's most recent book is *Tempo* (Puncher & Wattmann, 2013), which was shortlisted for the Prime Minister's Literary Awards and won the University of Melbourne Wesley Michel Wright Prize. She lives in Hobart where she teaches Year 12 Creative Writing. Her poems have been widely anthologised in Australia and overseas.

Joel Deane is a poet, novelist, journalist and speechwriter. His most recent collection of poetry, *Year of the Wasp* (Hunter Publishers), was published in May 2016.

Jelena Dinic arrived in Australia in 1993, during the collapse of Yugoslavia. She writes in Serbian and in English. Her poems and short stories have appeared in the *Australian Poetry Journal*, *Australian Book Review*, *Going Down Swinging* and many anthologies. Her chapbook *Buttons on my Dress* was published by Garron Publishing in 2015.

Dan Disney's most recent publications include *either, Orpheus* (UWAP, 2016) and *Report from a border* (with John Warwicker; Light-Trap Press, 2016). He currently teaches with the English Literature Program at Sogang University, in Seoul.

Lucy Dougan's books include *White Clay* (Giramondo, 2008) and *Meanderthals* (Web del Sol, 2012). Her latest book, *The Guardians* (Giramondo, 2015), was shortlisted for the 2015 Queensland premier's award for poetry and the 2016 Victorian and Western Australian premiers' awards for poetry. She lectures in Creative Writing at Curtin University and works for *Westerly*.

Laurie Duggan, born in Melbourne in 1949 and later a resident of Sydney and Brisbane, moved to Faversham, Kent, in 2006. His most recent books are *Allotments* (Bristol, Shearsman Books, 2014) and a reissue of his first two books as *East and Under the Weather* (Puncher & Wattmann, 2014).

Ali Cobby Eckermann is a poet and memoirist. Her collections of verse include *little bit long time* (Australian Poetry Centre, 2010), *Kami* (Vagabond Press, 2010) and *Love dreaming & other poems* (Vagabond Press, 2012). Her two verse novels are *His Father's Eyes* (Oxford University Press, 2011) and *Ruby Moonlight* (Magabala Books, 2012).

Stephen Edgar has published ten collections of poetry, the most recent being *Exhibits of the Sun* (Black Pepper, 2014), which was shortlisted for the Prime Minister's Literary Awards, as was his previous book, *Eldershaw* (Black Pepper, 2013). A new collection, *Transparencies*, is forthcoming.

Anne Elvey is the managing editor of *Plumwood Mountain*: *An Australian Journal of Ecopoetry and Ecopoetics*, and holds honorary appointments at Monash University and University of Divinity, Melbourne. Her recent publications include *Kin* (Five Islands, 2014), shortlisted for the Kenneth Slessor Poetry Prize 2015, and *This Flesh That You Know* (Leaf Press, 2015).

Michael Farrell is from Bombala, NSW and lives in Fitzroy, Melbourne. In 2015 he published *Cocky's Joy* (Giramondo) and *Writing Australian Unsettlement: Modes of Poetic Invention 1796–1945* (Palgrave Macmillan). Other books include *Open Sesame* (Giramondo, 2012), *A Raiders Guide* (Giramondo, 2008), *Break Me Ouch* (3deep Publishing, 2006) and *ode ode* (Salt Publishing, 2002), as well as several chapbooks. 'Death of a Year' is for Martin, and for the Slovene poet Tomaž Šalamun, both of whom died in 2014.

Liam Ferney's most recent collection is *Content* (Hunter Publishing, 2016). His second collection, *Boom* (Grand Parade Poets, 2013), was shortlisted for the NSW Premier's Poetry Prize and the Queensland Poetry Prize. He is a media manager, poet and aspiring left back living in Brisbane, Australia.

Toby Fitch is the poetry editor of *Overland*. His books include *Rawshock* (Puncher & Wattmann, 2012), which won the Grace Leven Prize for Poetry 2012, *Jerilderies* (Vagabond Press, 2014) and, most recently, *The Bloomin' Notions of Other & Beau* (Vagabond Press, 2016). His poem 'Janus' is an inversion of Arthur Rimbaud's 'Jeunesse'.

Lionel G. Fogarty is a Yugambeh man, born on Wakka Wakka land in South Western Queensland near Murgon on a 'punishment reserve'. Throughout the 1970s, he worked as an activist for Aboriginal Land Rights and protesting Aboriginal deaths in custody. He has published numerous collections of poetry, including most recently the award-winning *Connection Requital* (Vagabond Press, 2010) and *Mogwie-Idan: Stories of the land* (Vagabond Press, 2014).

Tina Giannoukos is a poet, writer, and reviewer. She has held a Varuna Fellowship, has lived and worked in Beijing, and has read her poetry in Greece and China. Her most recent collection is *Bull Days* (ASP/Arcadia, 2016).

Lisa Gorton lives in Melbourne and writes poetry, fiction and essays. Her two most recent publications, both with Giramondo, are the poetry collection *Hotel Hyperion* (2013) and a novel, *The Life of Houses* (2015). Her awards include the Victorian Premier's Prize for Poetry, the Philip Hodgins Memorial Medal and the NSW Premier's People's Choice Award for *The Life of Houses*.

Robert Gray was born in 1945 and lives in Sydney. His most recent books are *Coast Road: Selected Poems* (Black Inc., 2014), *Cumulus: Collected Poems* (John Leonard Press, 2013), and *The Land I Came Through Last* (Giramondo, 2008), a memoir.

Phillip Hall lives in Melbourne's Sunshine (western suburbs) where he works as a poet and reviewer. He is a very passionate member of the Western Bulldogs Football Club. He also continues, through his writing, to honour First Nations in the Northern Territory's Gulf of Carpentaria where he has family and friends.

Natalie Harkin is a Narungga woman, a member of the Chester family in South Australia. Her work is an archival-poetic journey that weaves a love of storytelling, activism and resistance-poetics through art and literature, to critically engage with the state's colonial archives. Her first collection is *Dirty Words* (Cordite Books, 2015).

Dennis Haskell is the author of eight collections of poetry, the most recent being *Ahead of Us* (Fremantle Press, 2016) and *What Are You Doing Here?* (University of The Philippines Press, 2015). He is a Member of the Order of Australia for 'services to literature, particularly poetry, to education and to intercultural understanding', and currently Chair of the Board of writingWA.

Dominique Hecq, born in the French-speaking part of Belgium, has spent most of her life in Australia. Her work crosses disciplines, genres and languages, resisting categorisation. She is the author of fifteen full-length works ranging from poetry, fiction and drama to books about creative writing informed by psychoanalysis. Having recently reconnected with her mother tongue, her works in progress include *Duel* (a bilingual collection) and *Envol d'aube*.

Paul Hetherington has published ten poetry collections, most recently *Burnt Umber* (UWAP, 2016), along with five chapbooks. He won the 2014 Western Australian Premier's Book Award (poetry) and was shortlisted for the 2013 Montreal International Poetry Prize. Recently he completed an Australia Council Residency in the B.R. Whiting Studio in Rome.

Fiona Hile's first full-length collection, *Novelties* (Hunter Publishers, 2013), was awarded the NSW Premier's Literary Awards Kenneth Slessor Prize for Poetry. She has been a recipient of the Gwen Harwood Poetry Prize and was awarded second place in the *Overland* Judith Wright Poetry Prize. Her second collection, *Subtraction*, will be published in 2016.

LK Holt lives in Melbourne. Her first collection of poems, *Man Wolf Man* (John Leonard Press, 2007), won the 2009 Kenneth Slessor Prize in the NSW Premier's Awards. *Patience, Mutiny* shared the 2011

Grace Leven Prize for Poetry. Her most recent collection is *Keeps* (John Leonard Press, 2014).

Andy Jackson's most recent collections are *Immune Systems* (Transit Lounge, 2015) and *That knocking* (Little Windows, 2016). *Music our bodies can't hold*, forthcoming from Hunter Publishers, consists of portrait poems of other people with Marfan Syndrome. He blogs about poetry and bodily otherness irregularly at amongtheregulars. wordpress.com.

Lisa Jacobson is the author of three books of poetry: *Hair & Skin & Teeth* (Five Islands Press, 1995); *The Sunlit Zone* (Five Islands Press, 2012), which won the Adelaide Festival John Bray Poetry Award and was shortlisted in four other national awards; and *South in the World* (UWAP, 2014). A new chapbook, *The Asylum Poems*, will be published in 2016.

Clive James, born and raised in Australia, has spent most of his career in England, but publishes prose and poetry all over the world. In the last few years he has been ill but continues to write, and among his publications in this later period have been a translation of Dante's *Divine Comedy*, two books of criticism, *Poetry Notebook* (Picador, 2014) and *Latest Readings* (YUP, 2015), and a collection of poems, *Sentenced to Life* (Picador, 2015). His *Collected Poems* was released in 2016 (Picador).

Virginia Jealous's travel journalism, essays and poems appear in publications in several countries. Her long-term obsession is with the extraordinary poet Laurence Hope – aka Violet Nicolson – who died in Madras in 1904. Virginia is based in Denmark, Western Australia.

A. Frances Johnson's poetry collections include *The Pallbearer's Garden* (Whitmore Press, 2008), and *The Wind-up Birdman of Moorabool Street* (Puncher & Wattmann, 2012), which received the 2012 Wesley Michel Wright Prize. In 2015 she was awarded the Griffith University Josephine Ulrick Prize. A third collection, *Rendition for Harp and Kalashnikov*, is forthcoming from Puncher & Wattmann.

Jill Jones' latest book, *The Leaves are My Sisters*, is part of a new chapbook series from Little Windows Press, Adelaide. Other recent books include *The Beautiful Anxiety* (Puncher & Wattmann, 2013), which won the 2015 Victorian Premier's Literary Award for Poetry, and *Breaking the Days* (Whitmore Press, 2015). She is a member of the J.M. Coetzee Centre for Creative Practice at the University of Adelaide.

Christopher (Kit) Kelen is a poet, scholar and visual artist, and Professor of English at the University of Macau, where he has taught Creative Writing and Literature for the last sixteen years. His poetry has been published in Chinese, Portuguese, French, Italian, Swedish, Indonesian and Filipino languages. Japanese and Greek collections are forthcoming. The most recent of Kelen's dozen English language books is *Scavenger's Season* (Puncher & Wattmann, 2014).

Cate Kennedy writes poetry, fiction and non-fiction and lives in the town of Castlemaine in Central Victoria. Her most recent poetry collection, *The Taste of River Water* (Scribe, 2011), received the Victorian Premier's Literary Award for Poetry. She works as a teacher and occasional editor, and is currently at work on an ambitious mutiple-viewpoint novel, which is proving a little troublesome.

John Kinsella is the author of many books of poetry, fiction and criticism. Recent poetry volumes are *Firebreaks* (WW Norton, 2016) and *Drowning in Wheat: Selected Poems* (Picador, 2016). John is a Fellow of Churchill College, Cambridge University, and Professor of Literature and Sustainability at Curtin University.

Andy Kissane's books include *Out to Lunch* (Puncher & Wattmann, 2015) and *Radiance* (Puncher & Wattmann, 2014), which was shortlisted for the Victorian and Western Australian premiers' prizes and the Adelaide Festival Awards. He was the winner of *Australian Poetry Journal's* 2015 Poem of the Year. His website is andykissane.com.

Shari Kocher is the author of *The Non-Sequitur of Snow* (Puncher & Wattmann, 2015). She holds a PhD from Melbourne University and currently works as a freelance editor, scholar and poet. See: carapacedreaming.wordpress.com.

Simeon Kronenberg has published poetry and essays in Australian poetry journals and anthologies, including *Australian Love Poems 2013, Meanjin, Southerly, Australian Poetry Journal, Contrappasso* and *Cordite Poetry Review*. In 2014 he won the Second Bite Poetry Prize. In 2015 he was shortlisted for the Newcastle Poetry Prize and in 2016 the Grieve Prize. He lives and works in Sydney.

Verity Laughton is a South Australian-based playwright and poet. She is currently undertaking a PhD in political theatre at Flinders University. Her most recent work was the verbatim theatre piece *The Red Cross Letters* in August, 2016.

Anthony Lawrence's most recent book is *Headwaters* (Pitt Street Poetry, 2016). His many awards include The Philip Hodgins Memorial Medal, the Blake Poetry Prize, the New South Wales Premier's Award, the Newcastle Poetry prize and the Josephine Ulrick Poetry Prize. He teaches Writing Poetry at Griffith University, Gold Coast, and lives at Hastings Point, NSW.

Bronwyn Lea's recent collections of poems include *The Deep North: A Selection of Poems* (Braziller 2013) and *The Other Way Out* (Giramondo 2008). She lives in Brisbane.

Emma Lew is from Melbourne. Her most recent publication is *Luminous Alias* (Vagabond Press, 2012).

Kate Lilley is Associate Professor of English and Director of Creative Writing at the University of Sydney. She is the author of *Versary* (Salt Publishing, 2002) and *Ladylike* (UWAP, 2012). *Versary* won the Grace Leven Prize and both books were shortlisted for the Kenneth Slessor Prize. Her new book, *Tilt*, is forthcoming with Vagabond Press in 2017.

Debbie Lim was born in Sydney and currently lives in Germany. Her poems have regularly appeared in *The Best Australian Poems*. Her chapbook *Beastly Eye* was published in 2012 (Vagabond Press).

Kate Llewellyn is the author of twenty-four books comprising eight of poetry, nine of memoir and four of travel as well as essays, nature writing and autobiography. She is the co-editor of *The Penguin Book of Australian Women Poets* (1986) and the author of the bestseller *The Waterlily: A Blue Mountains Journal* (Hudson Publishing, 1993). Her two latest books are *A Fig at the Gate* (Allen & Unwin, 2014), a book of nature writing, and *First Things First* (Wakefield Press, 2015), an anthology of her letters to friends.

Cameron Lowe lives in Geelong. His two book-length collections of poetry are *Porch Music* (Whitmore Press, 2010) and *Circle Work* (Puncher & Wattmann, 2013).

Jennifer Maiden has published twenty-two books – twenty poetry collections and two novels – many of which have won major awards. Her early novel *Play with Knives* (Allen & Unwin, 1990) has recently been re-published in a free online revised edition by Quemar Press (quemarpress.weebly.com).

Caitlin Maling is a WA poet. Her first collection *Conversations I've Never Had* (Fremantle Press, 2015), was shortlisted for the Mary Gilmore Award and the WA Premier's Awards. A second collection, *Border Crossing*, is scheduled for February 2017.

David Malouf is the author of poems, fiction, libretti and essays. In 1996, his novel *Remembering Babylon* was awarded the first International IMPAC Dublin Literary Award. His 1998 Boyer Lectures were published as *A Spirit of Play: The Making of Australian Consciousness* (ABC, 1998). In 2000 he was selected as the sixteenth Neustadt Laureate. His most recent novel is *Ransom* (Chatto & Windus, 2009).

David McCooey's latest collection of poems, *Star Struck*, was published in 2016 by UWA Publishing. His previous collection, *Outside*, (Salt Publishing, 2011), was shortlisted for the Queensland Literary Awards, and was a finalist for the Melbourne Prize for Literature's 'Best Writing Award'. David is a Professor of Writing and Literature at Deakin University in Geelong.

Kate Middleton is an Australian writer. She is the author of the poetry collections *Fire Season* (Giramondo, 2009), which was awarded the Western Australian Premier's Award for Poetry in 2009, and *Ephemeral Waters* (Giramondo, 2013), which was shortlisted for the NSW Premier's Award in 2014.

Peter Minter is a poet, poetry editor and writer on poetry and poetics. He teaches Indigenous Studies, Creative Writing and Australian Literature at the University of Sydney, and his most recent book, *In The Serious Light of Nothing*, was published by the Chinese University Press Hong Kong in 2013.

Les Murray lives in Bunyah, near Taree in New South Wales. He has published some thirty books. His work is studied in schools and universities around Australia and has been translated into several foreign languages. His collection *Waiting for the Past* (Black Inc., 2015) won the Queensland Premier's Literary Award and the Judith Wright Calanthe Award for poetry. His latest collection, *On Bunyah*, was published by Black Inc. in 2015.

π.o. Born: Katerini/Greece 1951. Came to Australia 1954. Raised: Fitzroy (inner suburb of Melbourne). Occupation: retired draughtsman i.e. now a Gentleman. By disposition and history is an Anarchist. Is currently editor of the experimental magazine UNUSUAL WORK. His latest book is *Fitzroy the biography* – an instant classic!

Ella O'Keefe is a poet and researcher living in Melbourne, Australia. She was the winner of the 2015 *Overland* Judith Wright Poetry Prize. Her poems have appeared in *Cordite Poetry Review*, *Steamer*, *Text Journal* and *Plumwood Mountain*. Her first chapbook, *Rhinestone*, was published by Stale Objects dePress in 2015. She has produced radio pieces for community and national broadcasters and is the Audio Producer for *Cordite Poetry Review*.

Meredi Ortega was born in Albany and grew up in Tom Price, WA. She won the Science Poetry Prize 2013 and came third in the Resurgence Poetry Prize 2015. She lives in Scotland.

Geoff Page has published twenty-two collections of poetry as well as two novels and five verse novels. His recent books include *1953* (UQP, 2013), *Improving the News* (Pitt Street Poetry, 2013), *New Selected Poems* (Puncher & Wattmann, 2013), *Aficionado: A Jazz Memoir* (Picaro Press, 2014), *Gods and Uncles* (Pitt Street Poetry, 2015), and *PLEVNA: A Verse Biography* (UWAP, 2016). He also edited *The Best Australian Poems 2014* and *The Best Australian Poems 2015* (Black Inc.).

Charmaine Papertalk-Green grew up in Mullewa and lives in Geraldton. She won the 2006 National NAIDOC Poster Competition for her work entitled *Life Circle*.

Felicity Plunkett's *Vanishing Point* (UQP, 2009) won the Arts Queensland Thomas Shapcott Prize and was shortlisted for several other awards. *Seastrands* (2011) was published by Vagabond Press. She is the editor of *Thirty Australian Poets* (UQP, 2011). Her poem 'What the Sea Remembers' was shortlisted in the 2015 Montreal International Poetry Prize.

Claire Potter is from Perth, Western Australia. She has published two chapbooks, *In Front of a Comma* (Poets Union, 2006), and *N'ombre* (Vagabond Press, 2007), and a full-length collection, *Swallow* (Five Islands, 2010). She lives in London.

Hessom Razavi is a doctor and writer who grew up in Tehran, Karachi, Manchester and Perth. His poetry has featured in *Gargouille*, *Mascara Literary Review* and the Hippocrates Prize for Poetry and Medicine. He is currently working on his first collection.

Peter Rose is the author of six poetry collections, the most recent being *The Subject of Feeling* (UWAP, 2015). His family memoir, *Rose Boys* (Allen & Unwin, 2001), has now been published as a Text Classic.

Robyn Rowland has nine books of poetry, including *Line of Drift* (Doire Press, Ireland, Irish Arts Council sponsored, 2015), and the bilingual *This Intimate War Gallipoli/Çanakkale 1915 – İçli Dışlı Bir Savaş: Gelibolu/Çanakkale 1915*, Turkish translation by Mehmet Ali Çelikel (Five Islands Press, Australia; Bilge Kultur Sanat, Turkey; Municipality of Çanakkale sponsored, 2014).

Gig Ryan's seventh book, *New and Selected Poems* (Giramondo, 2011; *Selected Poems*, Bloodaxe Books, UK), was winner of the 2012 Grace Leven Prize for Poetry and the 2012 Kenneth Slessor Prize for Poetry. She has also written songs with Disband – 'Six Goodbyes' (1988) – and Driving Past – 'Real Estate' (1999) and 'Travel' (2006). She is Poetry Editor of the *Age* and a freelance reviewer, and is working on another book of poems.

Tracy Ryan is a Western Australian poet who has also lived for long periods overseas. Her latest book of poems is *Hoard* (Whitmore Press, 2015). Her most recent novel is *Claustrophobia* (Transit Lounge, 2014). She has a new novel forthcoming, also with Transit Lounge.

Omar Sakr is an Arab–Australian poet. His poetry has appeared most recently in *Strange Horizons*, *Going Down Swinging*, *Overland*, and *Meanjin*, among others. He was awarded the runner-up prize in this year's Judith Wright Poetry Prize, and his debut collection, *these wild houses*, is forthcoming from Cordite Books (2017).

Jaya Savige grew up on Bribie Island, Queensland. He is the author of *Latecomers* (UQP, 2005), *Surface to Air* (UQP, 2011) and a chapbook,

Maze Bright (Vagabond Press, 2014). He read for a PhD on James Joyce at the University of Cambridge, and currently lives in London.

Thomas Shapcott has published 15 collections of poems, as well as eight novels and over 20 libretti. Translations of his work in book form have been published in Hungary, Romania and the Republic of Macedonia. In 1989 he was awarded an Order of Australia for services to literature and in 2000 he won the Patrick White Award. The Arts Queensland Thomas Shapcott Poetry Prize was named in his honour. He lives in Melbourne.

Alex Skovron's sixth and most recent collection, *Towards the Equator: New & Selected Poems* (Puncher & Wattman, 2014), was shortlisted in the Prime Minister's Literary Awards. A volume of short stories, *The Man who Took to his Bed*, is forthcoming from Puncher & Wattmann. He lives in Melbourne and works as a freelance editor.

Maria Takolander's most recent poetry collection is *The End of the World* (Giramondo, 2014). She is also the author of *The Double* (Text, 2013), which was shortlisted for the 2015 Melbourne Prize for Literature. She is an Associate Professor in Writing and Literature at Deakin University in Geelong, Victoria.

Tim Thorne lives in Launceston, Tasmania. The latest of his fourteen collections of poetry is *The Unspeak Poems and other verses* (Walleah Press, 2014). He has twice been a finalist in the National Poetry Slam. In 2012 he won the Christopher Brennan Award and in 2014 the Gwen Harwood Prize.

John Tranter has won many Australian poetry prizes and has published over twenty books, including *Starlight* (UQP, and BlazeVox Books, Buffalo, USA, 2010), and *Heart Starter* (Puncher & Wattmann, and BlazeVox Books, Buffalo, USA, 2015). He is the founder of the Australian Poetry Library (poetrylibrary.edu.au), of *Jacket magazine* (jacketmagazine.com), and of *Journal of Poetics Research* (poeticsresearch.com). He has a WordPress journal at johntranter.net, and a static HTML homepage at johntranter.com.

Ellen van Neerven is a Yugambeh woman living in Brisbane. Her debut work of fiction, *Heat and Light*, has won several prestigious awards. *Comfort Food*, her first poetry collection, was published by UQP in 2016.

Ann Vickery is a Senior Lecturer in Writing and Literature at Deakin University. She is the author of *Devious Intimacy* (Hunter Publishers, 2015), *The Complete Pocketbook of Swoon* (Vagabond Press, 2014), *Stressing the Modern: Cultural Politics in Australian Women's Poetry* (Salt Publishing, 2007) and *Leaving Lines of Gender: A Feminist Genealogy of Language Writing* (Wesleyan University Press, 2000).

Chris Wallace-Crabbe lives in Brunswick. He taught literature for many years at Melbourne University, and also overseas. Mainly a poet, he also collaborates on artists' books, most recently *Imagined Cities* (NGV, 2016) with Jan Senbergs. His latest books of poetry are *My Feet Are Hungry* (Pitt Street Poets, 2014) and *Afternoon in the Central Nervous System* (George Braziller, 2015).

Simon West is a poet and Italianist, and Honorary Fellow in the School of Languages at the University of Melbourne. He is the author of three books of poetry, the most recent of which is *The Ladder* (Puncher & Wattmann, 2015), and a translation and critical edition of *The Selected Poetry of Guido Cavalcanti* (Troubadour, 2009).

Petra White works as a policy adviser. Her fourth collection of poetry is forthcoming from Gloria SMH in 2017.

Jessica L. Wilkinson is the founding editor of *Rabbit: a journal for nonfiction poetry*. She has published two poetic biographies, *marionette: notes toward the life and times of miss marion davies* (Vagabond Press, 2012) and *Suite for Percy Grainger* (Vagabond Press, 2014). She is a Senior Lecturer in Creative Writing at RMIT University, Melbourne.

Fiona Wright's book of essays, *Small Acts of Disappearance* (Giramondo, 2015), won the 2016 Kibble Award, and her poetry collection, *Knuckled* (Giramondo, 2011), won the 2012 Mary Gilmore Award. She has recently completed a PhD at Western Sydney University's Writing & Society Research Centre.

Ouyang Yu, now Professor of English at Shanghai University of International Business and Economics, has to date published 82 books of poetry, fiction, nonfiction, literary criticism and translation in English and Chinese. His latest book in Chinese is *A History of Literary Exchange between Australia and China* (Showwe Press, Taiwan, 2016).

Fay Zwicky began publishing poetry and short stories as an undergraduate at Melbourne University. She has been a concert pianist and was a Senior Lecturer in English literature at the University of Western Australia. She now devotes her time entirely to writing. Fay has received a number of awards for her writing. Her most recent publication with UQP is the collection *Fay Zwicky: Poems 1970–1992* (1993).

Billy Marshall Stoneking's first collection of poems, *Ear Ink* (Dead Center Vanity Press), appeared in 1979. A major collection, *Singing the Snake: Poems from the Western Desert 1979–1988*, was published by Angus & Robertson in 1990. With Eric Beach and others, he was involved in the foundation of the Poets Union of Australia. He was also involved in the performance poetry scene, and featured in the performance poetry anthology *Off the Record*, edited by π.o. (1985). Billy died in July 2016.